The Mahabodhi Temple at Bodh Gaya

The Mahabodhi Temple at Bodh Gaya

PROF. RYOJUN SATO

MOTILAL BANARSIDASS PUBLISHERS
PRIVATE LIMITED • DELHI

2nd Reprint : Delhi, 2019
First Edition : Delhi, 2014

ISBN: 978-81-208-3943-4 (Cloth)
ISBN: 978-81-208-4025-6 (Paper)

Also available at

MOTILAL BANARSIDASS

41 U.A. Bungalow Road, Jawahar Nagar, Delhi 110 007
1 B, J S Compound, Kennedy Bridge, Nana Chowk, Mumbai 400 007
203 Royapettah High Road, Mylapore, Chennai 600 004
49, 8th F Main III Block, Jayanagar, Bengaluru-560 011
9, Panchanan Ghosh Lane, 1st Floor, Kolkata 700 009
Ashok Rajpath, Patna 800 004
Chowk, Varanasi 221 001

MLBD Cataloging-in-Publication Data
The Mahabodhi Temple at Bodh Gaya by Ryojun Sato
Includes 4 Appendices and Bibliography
ISBN: 978-81-208-3943-4 (Cloth)
ISBN: 978-81-208-4025-6 (Paper)
I. The Mahabodhi Temple II. Bodh Gaya
III. Sato Ryojun

Printed in India

by RP Jain at NAB Printing Unit,
A-44, Naraina Industrial Area, Phase I, New Delhi–110028
and published by JP Jain for Motilal Banarsidass Publishers (P) Ltd,
41 U.A. Bungalow Road, Jawahar Nagar, Delhi-110007

Contents

Foreword

The Mahabodhi Mahavihara which stands majestically identifying the spot of the Buddha's Enlightenment is not only an artistic edifice but is also a place of worship where people and practitioners have immense faith and belief and also is a cultural landmark which identifies itself with the message of the master with that of love and compassion, equanimity and sacrifice, unity and brotherhood.

People, believers, practitioners and adherers all come here to offer their venerations not only to the sacred Bodhi Tree or the Vajrasana or the Temple itself but come here for meditation and seeking that illusive peace and tranquillity as the Buddha Himself advised His faithfuls that at least once in their lifetime one should go on a pilgrimage to the four holy places connected with the life of the Buddha which are Lumbini—where Prince Siddhartha Gautama was born, Buddhagaya—where Siddhartha Gautama attained Enlightenment to become the Buddha, Sarnath—where the Buddha for the first time preached the Dhammacakkapavattana Sutra or turning of the wheel of Dhamma and Kusinagar—where the Buddha entered into mahaparinibbana. His advice to His followers to go on a pilgrimage was much as to gather inspiration for their practice but at the same time was an occasion to meet many more monks and other faithfuls from whom one could share their experiences and learn more about the Dhamma.

One of the earliest pilgrims who came here to visit the place after the Buddha's demise was none other than King Asoka the Great (273–232) of Pataliputra which happened 250 years after the Masters demise. This visit brought glamour, importance, state sponsorship and laid the foundation of this place when he constructed the Vajrasana and a Stupa marking the spot of the Buddha's Enlightenment. Prior to his visit it is recorded that Kurangi and Nagadevi had constructed railings around the Bodhi Tree. But it was the visit of Asoka and his subsequent visits that made this place important in the annals of history.

The present Mahabodhi Temple was built in the 2nd century AD and built over the original stupa constructed by King Asoka. It was during the Gupta reign that the magnificent Temple was completed in around 7th century AD. The awe generating gilded statue that we see inside the shrine room was made some time in the year 380 AD. It is made of black stone and painted in gold which is of recent practice. Such was the awe generated from the sublimity of the Buddha statue that when the Noble Laureate Rabindranath Tagore visited the Mahabodhi Temple it was the first time in his life that he felt like bowing his head in front of a statue.

The Bodhi Tree under which the Buddha attained Enlightenment has its own history. Although it is a tree revered and worshipped by the millions around the world, the faithful seek from it solace and peace sitting under its widely spread branches. This tree which stands today is not the original one but is a descendant of the original. It was Asoka's son Mahendra and daughter Sanghamitra who had taken a sapling of this sacred tree to Sri Lanka as a gift from the King Asoka as a token of his admiration for the people of that country and opening a chapter in his foreign policy, it has today become a symbol of our friendship between both the countries. The present tree is the 4th or 5th tree in succession. Although there are myths and legends and heresays about the tree over the centuries but this tree remains the cynosure of all eyes and steadfast dedication and unwavering faith irrespective of nationalities and creeds. No Buddhist can ever dream of causing harm to the tree but will do all that is needed to safeguard the tree and ensure its longevity especially when we know that the life span of the ficus religiosa or the peepul tree is very short but a fast growing tree and easily grows needing not much support or help during its growth. It is a matter of significance that the Bodhi Tree of Anuradhapura has gone on to become the oldest recorded tree in the world.

There is no recorded history in continuity from the earliest times to the present day. It is the travelogues of Fa Hien or Fu Xian (337–424), Xuạn Zang (600–664) and It-sing (671–695) which gives us a vivid picture of the place and time to deconstruct the history of the place, in fact the entire Buddhist landscape. Dr. B. M. Barua's monumenral work *Gaya and Buddhagaya: Early History of the Holy Land* in two volumes, Alexander Cunningham's *Mahabodhi or the Great Buddhist Temple under the Bodhi Tree at Buddha Gaya*, Dr. Rajendra Lal Mitra's *Buddhagaya: The Great Buddhist Temple* also count amongst the documentation of this place. Prof. Dipak Kumar Barua has attempted with his *Buddha Gaya Temple: Its History* which deals with the history of the place in detail but the attempt made by Prof Ryojun Sato brings to light the history of this place divided into chapters and giving in detail from multiple sources which makes it for easier comprehension dealing minutely which is not available otherwise.

Buddhagaya has changed a lot over the years and is changing everyday to meet the demands of the times. Although archaeologists will argue that this is an archaeological monument but we should not forget that this is also a living temple where people have immense faith and belief. Due to the increase in pilgrims arrival it is imperative to provide infrastructural support like pathways, toilets, refreshing rooms, meditation places, place to light lamps and incense, space for pujas and a serene environment commensurate with the other religious and spiritual centres. After being declared a World Heritage Property by UNESCO the place started to receive more attention. With the airport coming up at Gaya arrival of pilgrims increased manifold and with better connectivity by road and rail people have far more options to travel than what was available 15 years back. The township requires infrastructure support like drainage and sewerage, cleanliness and garbage disposal mechanism, pure drinking water, tourist friendly bus and taxi stands, shopping complexes and regulated markets, undergroumd cable electrification. The Administration has to also look into the aspect of local transportation catering to the domestic populace.

Buddhagaya has in the modern period received attention in the year 1956 when India was celebrating the 2500 Buddha Jayanti whereas it should have been the 2500th Buddha's mahaparinirvana. The celebrations were organised by the Government of India under the leadership of the honourable Prime Minister Pandit Jawaharlal Nehru who advocated the necessity of the Buddha's teachings and revival of the places of Buddhist interest connected with the life of the Buddha. He urged the Buddhist countries to construct Buddhist viharas and monasteries in Buddhagaya depicting their art and architecture, their cultural ethos which in turn would contribute to the cultural legacy of this place. Today we have viharas of all the Buddhist countries which have enriched Buddhagaya into a cultural repository. Alongwith these viharas they brought with them their food habits and clothing, their language and their style. But what is important with this place is that with the advent of the Muslim rule in the 12th century AD Buddhism went into a decline due to man made miseries and then the natures fury. Buddhist monks either had to flee or had to convert and this had left a vacuum here and the place left abandoned. Subsequent years of neglect over the centuries made the Mahabodhi Mahavihara look like a skeleton until interest in it was rekindled by Sir Edwin Arnold (1832–1904) through his writings and exhortations to the Buddhist world to come and see for themselves in what utter ruins the Temple was in. This call of his was echoed in Sri Lanka when a young man named Don David Hewawitharane who went on to become the Anagarika Dharmapala (1864–1933) came to Buddhagaya and stayed back vowing to restore the sacred site and also to give to the Buddhists the right of worship. To achieve this cause he instituted the Maha Bodhi Society of India (1891) whose headquarters he shifted to Calcutta for better coordination. The Temple having been abandoned by the Buddhists after the Muslim invasion was left with no care or legitimate heir and a Saivite wandering ascetic finding it to be a nice and peaceful abode took shelter there and over a long period of his stay his disciples and heirs—the Mahants went on to become one of the biggest landlords of the place or the entire state. They created vast tracts of agricultural lands and estates and controlled everything from the lives of the people to the economy of the place, the law of the place and the religious spectre of the area. Such was their might that their writ ran far and large and the effect was felt by Anagarika Dharmapala when he was obstructed and abused and beaten by the Mahant and his men from even entering the Temple. The Anagarika was assisted in his struggle by numerous monks and the laity and few amongst them are such protagonists like Ven. Matale Sumangala, Ven. Dunuvila Chandajoti, Ven. Anuradhapure Pemananda, Ven. Galle Sudassana of Sri Lanka and Ven. Shaku Kozen of Yokohama, Japan. He received impetus from the important luminaries of that time and few amongst them were Ven. Kripasaran Mahasthavir (1864–1926) Founder of the Bengal Buddhist Association (1892 and contemporary of the Anagarika, Sir Asutosh Mookerjee (1864–1924) who was the Vice Chancellor of the Calcutta University to whom goes the credit of reviving Pali Studies in schools and colleges and it was his initiative of sending Dr. B. M. Barua (1888–1948) to the University of London for his higher studies when he went on to become the first Asian to receive the D. Lit. Degree from the University. After a protracted legal battle and political brinksmanship the issue was half settled when the Government of India and the Government of Bihar brought in a Bill in the Bihar Legislative Assembly titled "The Bodhgaya Temple Act of 1949" which gave the rights of management of the Shrine to a Committee constituted by the Act named the *Bodhgaya Temple Management Committee* with 4 Hindu members and 4 Buddhist members with the District Magistrate of Gaya being the Chairman provided he or she is a Hindu. In 2013 this Act was amended to provide that the District Magistrate of Gaya to be the Chairman no matter he comes from any religious denomination. Keeping the concerns of the Buddhist community in mind the Act had provision for the *Bodhgaya Temple Advisory Board* with three fourths of the members being Buddhists made up by the Ambassadors and High Commissioners of the Buddhist countries and Buddhists from India and the rest being the local Member of the Legislative Assembly, Member of Parliament, officers from the local administration, the Chairman of the BTMC and the Commissioner of Magadh Division being the Member-Secretary.

The management of the Shrine has become more challenging than ever before as all eyes are rivetted on it by believers and faithfuls as well as tourists and visitors. The management has to deal with multiple demands and sentiments and above all the safety, security and sanctity of the place. The recent bomb explosions that have taken place in the Mahabodhi Mahavihara are an eye opener to all of us as to what can happen and how nasty a beating it can take. Yet the Mahabodhi is a place of worship and meditation, a spot of veneration and spirituality to millions of devotees and faithfuls will keep standing tall. We know from history that to save the Bodhi Tree from danger the King Purnavarna built a wall as high as 30 feet around the tree and now we are all seeing walls being erected around the Temple to save it from any external danger that has signalled with that of the blasts.

Prof. Rev. Ryojun Sato, Professor Emeritus of the Taisho University, Tokyo, and Chief Priest, Koen-ji Temple, Tokyo, Japan has done a commendable job by writing on this topic and saw his enthusiasm when he came researching to Buddhagaya to find out more details of the site and I have been of little help when I was engaged with the Mahabodhi Mahavihara which provides me satisfaction to be of use in this journey. Prof. Sato is an old India hand having done his research in 1956 in Delhi University when all things from food to lodging to transport were all so modest and yet he did not waver to complete his education. I wish him a fruitful life and more scholarly pursuits to leave for us as I do believe he is one of the very few scholars left who are sure intellectuals of their era. I am sure this book will also prove to be useful to the readers as well as the researchers and scholars to know more about the Mahabodhi Mahavihara and Buddhagaya as a whole. Being a busy person as he is and old with age and experience I offer my thanks to him for publishing this book.

Bhikkhu Bodhipala

Former Chief Priest, Mahabodhi Mahavihara
Principal, Kripasaran Continental Institution, Kolkata
Governing Body Member, Maha Bodhi Society of India
Asst. Secretary, International Brotherhood Mission, Assam

1 The Distant Past

The history of the religious center Bodh Gaya, in Bihar, India, where Shakyamuni is said to have attained enlightenment as a Buddha, can be traced to the Neolithic Age, long before the time of Shakyamuni himself.

The site of what are called the Taradih remains stretches southwest and north of the Bodh Gaya Mahabodhi Great Stupa, 600 meters east to west and 500 meters north to south. The site's present name is thought to be based on that of a Hindu goddess called Tara. Located to the right of the Great Stupa entrance, Taradih now consists of no more than scattered brick-masonry remnants in a poor state of post-excavation preservation. A mosque has been built on part of the site. Today Taradih is eight meters above the level of Phalgu riverbed, but traces indicate frequent past flood-related inundations. Chronologically, the site is valuable evidence indicating a continuous cultural epoch extending from the Neolithic Age to the time of the Pala dynasty (750–1174). Its excavation could not begin until after the removal of earth piled there by the British archaeologist Alexander Cunningham when he excavated the Mahabodhi Great Stupa. Meade started excavating the Great Stupa core in 1861. In 1880, J.D. Beglar had already brought to light such important elements as the Seat of Enlightenment called the Diamond Throne (Vajrasana). But at Taradih itself, in 1981–82, laying out four trenches, Ajit K. Prasad clearly established

The Taradih remains

a chronology beginning with the Neolithic Age, continuing through the time of Shakyamuni, and extending to the age of Pala dynasty. This chronology consists of seven periods (Period 1: Neolithic Age. Period 2: Chalcolithic Age, sometimes black-rimmed red ware with white markings and soapstone beads. Period 3: Introduction of ironware; traces of unhulled rice; various ceramics including black-rimmed red ware, black ware, and red ware; plus diverse bodily ornaments. Period 4: Predominantly northern black polished ware (NBPW),* clay figurines and body ornaments. Period 5: SungaKushana dynasties. Period 6: Gupta and later Gupta dynasties. Period 7: Pala dynasty).

Lasting until 1985, excavations unearthed many artifacts including unglazed-pottery and stone body ornaments, clay figurines, Buddha statuettes, and stone Buddha figures. In 1988, artifacts from the NBPW period to the time of the Pala dynasty were discovered in the rear of the site of the nearby Samanvay Ashram.

According to Buddhist documents, in the time of Shakyamuni, Bodh Gaya was an important base for Jatila fire worshippers. The assertion is interestingly substantiated by the discovery of many fire guards at Taradih. This may relate to the tradition of the conversion of the three Kassyapa brothers, who, before putting their faith in Shakyamuni, had performed ceremonies using fire. Gaya, where Shakyamuni exorcised the fire-spewing Naga serpent, is close. The statement in the

Mahavamsa (The great chronicle), a history of Sri Lanka, to the effect that, at the period in question, pot production flourished in this region agrees with the large quantities of pottery shards of various forms, colors, and constructions discovered there. Dr. Prasad of the Patna Museum, who has excavated in this region for many years, described Taradih as the only site where it is possible to see artifacts from a continuous cultural epoch extending from the Neolithic Age to the time of the Pala dynasty not only from the State of Bihar, but also from all of India and the Asian Continent.

The relation between Taradih and the Great Stupa is totally unknown. The *Mahavamsa* states that a Brahman born near a tree at Mahabodhi studied the Three Vedas and acquired knowledge and skills. Although a later work, the *Gaya Mahatmya* (Glory of Gaya), which gives an account of the sacred region of Gaya, is thought to contain historical facts. It records mention of the Bodhi Tree.

Reliefs on the Bharhut stupa, thought to have been built in the first century B.C., depict the Bodhi Tree; and the *Kalingabodhi Jataka* (*Jataka Tales*), one of the tales of the previous lives of Shakyamuni, mentions the *bodhimanda* or place of enlightenment.

Though all of these references remain within the realm of tradition, they provide valuable material about Bodh Gaya as the place where Shakyamuni attained enlightenment.

*Northern black polished ware (NBPW, sometimes NBP). Hard black ceramic figurines, vessels, and jars distributed along the Ganges in northern India. Because the times of its production are known, it is useful in ascertaining historical periods.

2 Donation Inscription of the Noble Lady Kurangi

The first archaeological record relating to the building of the Bodh Gaya Great Stupa is found in the four letters of the words Ayya Kurangi. Kurangi is thought to be a woman's name. The title *Ayya* indicates that the lady was the wife of a monarch or person of authority. The inscription was carved at the time when this noble lady donated the railing to the temple. The real railing has been moved to the Archaeological Museum, Bodh Gaya. The one positioned at the stupa is a replica. The inscription is written in Ashoka Brahmi letters. It is thought that the Lady Kurangi may have lived during the Sunga dynasty (first century B.C.). But, since this is not certain, it is impossible to say when the Great Stupa was built. On the basis of other stupas in different parts of India, it is likely that initially this was a small mound or brick memorial tower. As fired bricks came to be used in place of sun-dried bricks, the scale of such towers increased.

In ancient India gifts to shrines and temples often bore donors' names and the purpose of the gift as, for example, a memorial of one's parents. In later period, inscribed names of monarchs and people of power were accompanied by numerous titles like king, king of kings, great king, or monarch filled with compassion. Incidentally, Shakyamuni himself has 12 titles including Teacher of Heavenly and Human Beings.

Donors are frequently represented in person. For

instance the relief at Bharhut, showing Buddhist lay disciple Anathapindika, who donated the Jeta Grove to the Order, is well known. He occupies a central position in the relief and holds a water phial. A man and wife who were donors appear in life-size representation at the entrance to the Karla caves in the Ghats Mountains of western India.

The meanings of early inscriptions, which consist of names plus two or three lines of simple explanation, are frequently unclear. Consequently, determining historical period must be judged from considerations of such other things as the nature of the stone, characteristics of the lettering, comparisons with other inscriptions, mention in scriptures, and so on. Not all inscriptions are read from top line downward. Some begin at the bottom line and move upwards. Some, like Ashoka Brahmi texts, are read from the left, whereas many in northwestern India are of the Aramaic system, which is read right to left.

Two lines inscribed on the railing coping slightly clarify the identity of Kurangi: "The gift of Kurangi, the daughter of Jiva, the sister-in-law of Indragnimitra, the son of ——." Since it was the custom with such inscriptions to give one's genealogy in detail, the name of a sister-in-law is revealed.

Nothing exact is known about the origin of the Great Stupa. In his Seventh Rock Inscription the following is said about King Ashoka: "But 10 years after Beloved-of-the-Gods had been crowned, he went on a tour to Sambodhi." The date referred to corresponds to 260 B.C., and it is though that Ashoka actually made the pilgrimage. The Bodhi tree is referred to as *bodhidruma* or *bodhivriksha*. The *Mahavamsa* gives the 18th year after his coronation as the time of the pilgrimage, and the *Dipavamsa* (Chronicle of the island) says he was guided in his travel by the high-ranking priest Upagupta.

Both histories append several episodes for none of which corroborating historical records exist. Visiting the locale in the seventh century, the Chinese monk Xuanzang (c.600–664),

An offering of the Noble Lady Kurangi. The second line is a different inscription.

wrote that Ashoka had built a small monastery, which a later Brahman enlarged into a great monastery.

Alexander Cunningham said that the site of the Buddhas enlightenment was probably the Bodhi tree itself surrounded by railings like the one shown being worshipped by believers in the first-century B.C. railing relief at Bharhut.

Though he visited the place in the fifth century, another Chinese monk Faxian (337424) makes no mention of the Great Stupa in his *Foguo ji(Record of Buddhist Kingdoms*). In the seventh century, Xuanzang, however, gives a detailed explanation of it in his *Datang xiyu ji* (*Great Tang Records on the Western Regions*). One scholarly theory contends that the stupa must have been built in the years between the visits of these two pilgrims. Others argue that Faxian intentionally said nothing about it.

The pedestal of a Buddha statue found outside the south gate of the Great Stupa is from the later Indo-Scythian period or the Gupta dynasty and is inscribed with the date Vikram Samvat* 64, which corresponds to 152, during the time of King Huviska. Damage to the inscription obscures the name of the donor, but the discovery of five punch marked coins in the second and third centuries support this dating.

Although many have been lost, it is believed that inscriptions of donors names were engraved without a break from age to age. Moreover, possibly as a result of Indian attitude toward history, no accounts remain of people who lived at the Great Stupa or of the annual events occurring there.

Some of the inscriptions from the Indo-Scythian period (150–c.600) are lengthy.

Though it is considerably weathered, the inscription on the north side (inner side) of the coping on the south side can be read as follows: "The Diamond Throne of the great Gandakuti Temple was made at ——." *Gandakuti* means living quarters where the Buddha actually resided. Later it came to mean the general residential zone of a temple.

The inscription continues: "Moon, sun, stars —— Vihara Buddha statue," indicating that it was used during enshrinement of a great temple and Buddha statue. The inscription dates from the second century, the time of the Indo-Scythian King Huvishka. An inscription from the Gupta period—fifth century—mentions pilgrims' donating money for votive lamps.

***Vikram Samvat is a distinctive Indian calendar differing by 56 or 57 years from the Western calendar.**

3 The Sujata Tradition I

Shakyamuni's six years of ascetic practices in the search for enlightenment ended fruitlessly. Realizing that such was not the correct way to enlightenment, Shakyamuni descended the Pragbodhi Hill, cleansed his body in the waters of the Nairanjara River, and sat in profound meditation under a Bodhi tree on the river bank. At this time, a herd maiden from Sena in the village of Uruvela offered him some milk gruel. Upon eating it, he was restored in spirit and body. And, as many Buddhist traditions relate, he attained enlightenment on December 8 as the morning star was shining. Most Japanese traditions refer to the maiden who offered the milk gruel only as the herd girl Sujata. A careful examination of the scriptures, however, uncovers various opinions.

For example, the *Nidanakatha* introduction to the *Jataka Tales*, which relate earlier existences of Shakyamuni (referred to in these stories as the Bodhisattva), makes mention of a marriageable girl named Sujata who was born into the house of a rich man of Senani in Uruvela. This young woman made a request of a certain *nyagrodha* or banyan tree: "If I marry into a lineage as good as my own, each year after the birth of my first son, I will bring as an offering to you 100 thousand gold coins."

When her prayer for a son was fulfilled, she milked one thousand cows, concentrated the milk, and poured it into a

Stupa on the site of Sujatas dwelling

pot on the very day when the Buddha was sensing enlightenment and about to enter Nirvana. Having resolved to become a Buddha without fail on that day, the Bodhisattva (Shakyamuni) was sitting under the tree. Sujatas maidservant Punna observed him and reported what she had seen to her mistress. Delighted, Sujata poured the milk gruel into a golden vessel and offered it to the Bodhisattva, whom she took to be the deity of the tree under which he sat. Clearly, joy that her prayer to the banyan tree for marriage and a son had been answered favorably caused Sujata to mistake Shakyamuni for the tree spirit and make her offering to him.

The popularity of tree worship in ancient India is apparent in Xuanzangs account of the origins of the city of Pataliputra in his *Great Tang Records on the Western Regions*. He writes that at a certain time and in a certain place, there lived a serious, studious young man who never indulged in pleasurable diversions. One day, however, some friends took him into the woods to have a good time. In jest, they pointed out a tree and told the young man that it was his wife and that he should take good care of her. Because, even when evening fell, he showed no signs of going home, the friends left him and returned themselves. But when several days passed and he still had not come home, they went to the forest where they found that the young man had married the spirit of the tree, built a splendid city bustling with people, and already had children. Since the tree of which the wife was the spirit was of a kind called a *patali*, the young man named the city Patalitputra, or child of Patali.

Other tales too mention trees in connection with Shakyamuni. For instance, one story relates how, after he had bathed in the river but was too weak from ascetic practices to climb from the water himself, a female tree deity on the bank stretched out her hand to help him. Forbidden to touch women, however, he refused her aid. According to a yet another surviving tale, when as a child he went to the fields to watch an agricultural festival, the trees shifted their branches from east to west to block the sun.

The legend of Sujata's mistaking Shakyamuni for a tree deity belongs in this same current, though it appears only in the "Tale of Cause and Effect" in the Pali Jatakas.

The *Mahavastu* (The great event) contains another tradition according to which Sujata, as the mother of the Bodhisattva (Shakyamuni) in an earlier life, stood holding milk gruel at the base of a banyan tree.

A version in which two herding maidens offer rice gruel to Shakyamuni occurs in numerous scriptures. In at least seven places—the section on taking up the monastic life, the section on causing disunity in the community of the Order, and a miscellany section—the *Mulasaravastivada-vinaya* relates a legend of two female donors offering rice gruel. Their names are Nanda and Nandapala. Without mentioning their names, the *Samyuktagama Yogacharya-sutra* also mentions two girls.

In *Faxian-chuan*, the Chinese monk Faxian (fourth and fifth centuries) writes of what he calls the Gramika girls as offering rice-and-milk gruel to the Buddha. The seventh-century-pilgrim Xuanzang records seeing a stupa on the site of the dwelling of the two herd girls who offered the milk gruel. From this reference, it is apparent that legends of two female donors were numerous. However, the scriptural location of the Gramika girls mentioned by Faxian is uncertain.

The *Lalitavistara-sutra* (*Extensive sport sutra*) lists the names of ten daughters of village chiefs who made offerings to the Bodhisattva, adding that Sujata, daughter of the chief of Nandika Village, filled a golden bowl with honeyed milk gruel and offered it to him.

4 The Sujata Tradition II

The Sujata Stupa, built on the site of her home, is across the river from the Mahabodhi Temple in the Bakraur district. Although in 1959 it was only a low hill covered with small trees, the construction of a low-water bridge across the river has made it readily accessible.

Excavations conducted by the Indian Archaeological Survey there in 1973–74 and again in 2001–06 uncovered a stupa with a round, two-level, terraced structure 11 meters high on a square east-west, north-south platform. The stupa reveals traces of three phases of additions and expansion from the Gupta to the Pala period. The first-phase, fired-brick, clockwise path around it is narrow with a surrounding wall of fired brick. Noteworthy traces indicate the existence of a wooden railing around the ground-level surrounding path.

In later expansions, this was widened to five meters and thickly covered in lime plaster. In third-phase expansions, a lime-plastered, fired-brick surrounding wall was added with railings on four sides and an open gate on each side. Between the surrounding wall and the gates a simple lime-plastered clockwise path was added. A fired-brick platform in front of one of the gates was probably used as a gathering place. The purpose of two brick constructions on the inner side of the gate is uncertain.

In the final phase of expansion, the stupa grew quite large,

Sujata herself might have walked through a market like this one at Bodh Gaya.

reaching a maximum diameter of 65.5 meters. Dating of the building and expansion of each level is unclear, but the initial phase of the residence site is thought to be from the second to the first century B.C. This estimation is made on the basis of shards of dark gray polished ceramic ware excavated from a building thought to be remains of a temple neighboring the stupa site on the northeast. Terracotta seals and small plaques reinforce the dating of the final expansion to from the eighth to the 10th century.

The attitudes of monarchs of the Pala dynasty toward Buddhism lead to the assumption that the surrounding walls, railings, and gates were erected in this period. An excavated inscription dating from the eight to the ninth century bearing the text The house of Sujata of King Devapala (ruled 810 to 850) makes it certain that the stupa was built as a memorial to Sujata. Also excavated from this locale are part of a golden earring, a small terracotta brooch, punch-marked coins, a stone Buddha head and torso, body ornaments, and terracotta seals.

Though names and numbers of the herd girl or girls who offered Shakyamuni milk gruel differ in various texts, the story is certainly not a total fabrication. Hinduism has also traditions about a starving god who is revived by drinking milk. In southern India, on festival days, Jains pour large quantities of milk on a great statue at Shravanabelagola. In India, dairy products are numerous, and milk is an important drink. The Sujata tradition can be considered an amalgam of faith in tree deities, Buddhist traditions, and emphasis on the importance of dairy products.

Belief in snakes was also popular in ancient times. This is illustrated by the experiences of Shakyamuni himself. After attaining enlightenment, he sat under the tree for seven days and seven nights enjoying his enlightened condition. When a violent storm blew up the serpent Muchalinda Naga coiled around him to provide protection.

Few relief carvings or paintings depict the legend of Sujata, though it plays a part in the large frescoes of the Buddha's life painted at the Horin-ji Temple (popularly known as the Nihon-ji) at Sarnath by the artist Kosetsu Nosu (1885–1973).

Before statues of the Buddha were produced, what is called a Buddha footprint was a major object of worship. There are many of them around the Great Stupa. Numerous Buddha-footprint stones remain in the vicinity of Sujata Village.

Worship of footprints persists at the Vishnupada Temple at Gaya, on the bank of the Phalgu River. A constant stream of people comes there to worship the footprint of the god Vishnu set in a hexagonal stone surround. Worshippers rubbing their heads against it and offerings of flowers and incense obscure the footprint from sight. Whether the worship of Vishnu's footprint or that of the Buddha started first is unknown.

The Bodhi tree in the precincts is said to be the actual one under which Shakyamuni attained enlightenment, although the figure beneath the tree represents a juvenile Vishnu. The temple is in fact a complex accommodating these two and the founding Jina of Jainism. Constantly burning crematory fires on the riverbed outside the temple are never allowed to go out, even when no cremation is in progress.

Reference: Fergusson, James: *Tree and Serpent Worship: Illustrations of Mythology and Art in India in the First and Fourth Centuries after Christ*

5 The Mahanama Dedicatory Inscription

Aside from others that are short and relatively unimportant, inscriptions clearly datable from the sixth century, in the time of the Gupta dynasty, include the Mahanama Dedication. There are two examples of inscriptions headed with the name *Mahanama*. The one called Mahanama II for the sake of convenience is long and written in the Gupta script of the latter half of the sixth century.

It is dated in this way: Chaturdashi the seventh day of the second week, the eve of the full moon, of the month Chaitra, in the year Samvat 269, thought to correspond to A.D. 588–89 (the date Samvat 269 is possibly an error).

Mahanama II was the author of the *Mahavamsa* (The great chronicle) and the uncle of Raja Dhatusena (459–77), who was regarded as the successor to Raja Mitrasena, killed by the invader Pandu in 433. Escaping with his uncle Mahanama, Dhatusena returned to defeat the invader and regain the throne in 459. During the ensuing 26 years, as the chief disciple of the exalted priest Upasena and a member of a powerful family, he lived in Amaradvipa on the island of Lanka. The inscription in question indicates that Mahanama II made a pilgrimage to the Bodhi tree in the kingdom of Magadha and donated a temple and Buddhist sculpture.

In the fifth century, the Chinese monk Faxian visited Bodh Gaya and recorded having seen three temples there. In

Representation of donors and an inscription inset into the floor of the Great Stupa

the seventh century, however, another Chinese monk named Xuanzang (602 64) put the number of temples at six. The temple architecture was probably commissioned by Raja Dhatusena (45977), the nephew of Mahanama II.

The gist of the inscription is as follows:

> Om! The righteous Law is eternally victorious. The Teacher of Humankind (one of the epithets of the Buddha), the head of the Shakya clan, shines like the full moon and is the foundation of all immeasurable existence. The Righteous Law is everywhere and ubiquitous. O, Teacher of Humankind, you who, by means of the Righteous Law and with logic as a weapon, have defeated all evils that, as warriors of heresy (non-Buddhist teachings), blocked the path to happiness and, resolutely standing up to them for the joy of all sentient beings, recovered the precious jewel of the Law stolen by the enemy!

It goes on to laud the revered sage and Buddha disciple Maha Kashyapa, whose protection is entreated and who is praised for abiding by the precepts fixed by the Teacher of Humankind and practicing the rules of precious meditation. He is said to bring desire under control by triumphing over the unbreakable suffering of existence and bringing liberation from the anguish of the cycle of reincarnations.

In this way, he embodied the mudra of meditation as indicated by the bodhisattva Maitreya.

It continues by saying that, after the Pure Buddha, the Most Honored of Two-legged Beings, had attained Nirvana, his disciples carried on his teachings. Purifying their senses and being compassionate to sentient beings, they traveled until finally arriving at the immaculate land at the foot of the Lanka mountains. The disciples who came after them were completely free of pride in worldly wealth.

The succession of generations of disciples included the *shramana* Bhava, who knew the happiness of meditation and who, able to tell good from evil, crushed error and came to possess the unparalleled treasure of the true Teachings. Rabuly was his disciple. Then came the ascetic Upasena, Mahanama I, and another Upasena.

This Upasena's disciple was Mahanama II, born on the island of Lanka and a resident of Amaradvipa. He built a beautiful mansion (temple) to the Teacher of Humankind, who overcame the power of Samara. It was as radiant as the moon and open on all four sides.

The merits or this act freed people from attachment to worldly things; dispelled mental darkness; and, like a torch, enabled them to enjoy the great happiness of perfect wisdom, clinging to nothing. As long as the sun, the dispeller of darkness, shines in all directions with its diffused rays; as long as the ocean is full of waves that are curled like the heads of dragons; and as long as Mount Sumeru, the abode of Indra, has its summit beautiful with various jeweled slabs so as to be full of luster, so long may this temple of the great Sage be everlasting.

> The seventh day in the moon-bright fortnight of the month of Chaitra in the year 279.

Dedicatory inscriptions of this length from ancient times are rare, though they become more numerous in later ages. Several of them engraved on copper plates survive.

6 Chinese Travel Journals: Faxian

Bodh Gaya inscriptions from the seventh and eighth centuries A.D. are limited in number, and it is not until the ninth-century Pala dynasty that dedicatory inscriptions appear again. For records on the Great Stupa in the interim period, we must rely on the travel diaries of Chinese monks and envoys. Of the monks traveling from China to India from the fourth to the eighth century, those whose names only are known number 169. In all likelihood, however, it may be presumed that several times that many made land or sea voyages there in search of the Buddhist Law.

Among their travel records, *Foguo ji* (*Record of Buddhist Kingdoms*) by Faxian (fourth and fifth centuries), *Datang xiyu ji* (*Great Tang Records on the Western Regions*) by Xuanzang (c.600–64), and *Nanhai ji gui nei fa zhuan* (*Account of Buddhism Sent from the South Seas*) by Yijing (653–713) are indispensable to comparative identifications of ruins and remains and verification of local customs and lifestyles. No scholar can avoid consulting the English translations of these documents by the oriental scholar Samuel Beal (1825–89).

Faxian was born during the Eastern Jin dynasty (307–420) in Shanxi. His three older brothers died young. In the hope of averting further similar calamity, his father devoted him to the religious life when he was three and had him accept monastic precepts when he was 20.

Aggrieved that the Buddhist monastic rules set forth in the *Vinaya Pitaka* had been only insufficiently transmitted to China, he requested to be allowed to go to India in search of the original texts. Thus, in March 399—when he was 64 years old—he set out from the Tang capital Changan with four companions, Huijing, Daojing, Huida, and Huigui. On their journey, they passed through Dunhuang, Shanshan, Khotan, and the Gandhara region. They crossed the Indus River in 403 and entered India from the northwest. After visiting sites associated with Shakyamuni such as Sravasti, Kushinagara (where the Buddha entered Nirvana), Pataliputra, and Rajagriha, they made a pilgrimage to Bodh Gaya.

On their return trip, traveling into eastern India from Benares, they made passage to Sri Lanka and, in 413, landed in Shantong Province, arriving in Nanjing (called Jiankang at that time). Visiting 27 countries over the 14 years of their major journey, they brought many Buddhist scriptures, including the Chinese *Mohosongzhi-lu* version of the *Mahasamghika Vinaya* and the *Mahisasaka Vinaya* (*Wufen-lu*).

At the end of the *Record of Buddhist Kingdoms*, Faxian wrote "After Fa-Hsien [Faxian] set out from Changan, it took him six years to reach Central India; (15) stoppages there extended over six (other) years; and on his return it took him three years to reach Ts'ing-chow (Qingzhou)." The dates of both his birth and death are uncertain.

It is thought that Faxian visited Bodh Gaya in 404. Of the experience he wrote as follows*:

> From Rajagriha, after traveling to the west for four *yojanas*, (the pilgrims) came to the city of Gaya; but inside the city all was emptiness and desolation. Going on again to the south for 20 *li* (one *li* equals about four kilometers), they arrived at the place where the Bodhisattva for six years practiced painful austerities.... Three *li* west from

here they came to the place where, when Buddha had gone into the water to bathe, a deva bent down the branch of a tree, by means of which he succeeded in getting out of the pool.

A Dharma-seeking priest (Collection of the Zojo-ji Temple)

Two *li* north from this was the place where the Gramika girls presented to Buddha the rice-gruel made with milk; and two *li* north from this (again) was the place where, seated on a rock under a great tree, and facing the east, he ate (the gruel). The tree and the rock are there at the present day. The rock may be six cubits in breadth and length, and rather more than two cubits in height.

After this, Faxian wrote that Shakyamuni intended to meditate and find enlightenment. But, at this moment, he wrote, devas told him, Less than half a *yojana* from this to the south-west will bring you to the *patra* tree, under which is the place for the attainment of enlightenment.

The Bodhisattva then arose and walked (after them). At a distance of 30 paces from the tree, a deva gave him the *kusa* grass of lucky omen (*Reineckia carnea*), which he received and went on. After (he had proceeded) fifteen paces, 500 green birds came flying towards him, went round him thrice, and disappeared. The Bodhisattva went forward to the *patra* tree, placed the *kusa* grass at the foot of it, and sat down with his face to the east. Then king (demon) Mara sent three beautiful young ladies, who came from the north, to tempt him, while the king himself came from the south to do the same. The Bodhisattva put his toes down on the ground, and the demon soldiers retired and dispersed, and the three young ladies were changed into old (grand-)mothers. At the place mentioned above of the six years' painful austerities, and at all these other places, men subsequently reared stupas and set up images, which all exist at the present day.

Faxian further visited the place where Shakyamuni sat for seven days and seven nights enjoying his enlightened condition while the Naga Raja Muchilinda protected him, where Brahma Deva requested him to share his teachings, where the Four Devas brought him their alms bowls, where 500 merchants offered him honey, and where he converted the three Kasyapa brothers and their one thousand followers. Faxian wrote that stupas had been erected at all of these places.

He adds emphatically that monks reside in the three temples; that the local residents are generous in making offerings; that the precepts are observed; and that dignity is preserved in rising, abiding, and entering the group (human relations), just as they were when Shakyamuni was alive. Next he mentions four great topes. Then we read that, after crossing Mount Gurupada, he returned to Pataliputra.

He is silent, however, about the size or scale of the Bodh Gaya Great Stupa, and all he says about the four great topes is that they were erected at places connected with Shakyamuni's life and enlightenment. It is uncertain whether the Great Stupa did not exist when he visited Bodh Gaya or whether for some reason he deliberately refrained from mentioning it.

***English text based on translations by James Legge (1815–97).**

7 Chinese Imperial Envoy: Wang Xuance I

The pre-Christian-era Indian practice of leaving inscriptions undated makes establishing chronologies difficult and differs greatly from the approach of the Chinese, who, from the beginning of the historical era, have scrupulously recorded dates and names. Chinese travel journals and Chinese-language inscriptions are therefore an indispensable aid to the chronology of the Bodh Gaya Great Stupa and other Buddhist sacred places.

Sino-Indian relations started at the time when the people the Chinese called the Da Yuezhi (Great Yuezhi) controlled the northwestern part of the Indian subcontinent. According to the *Weishu* (Book of Wei) 114, in the year 2 B.C., the king of the Yuezhi had an emissary named Yicun carry to China a book recording the achievements of bodhisattvas, *sravakas* (hearers of the Dharma), and *bhikkhus* (monks). The Da Yuezhi king at the time was Kujala Kadphises who had "Preserver of the True Teaching" stamped on some of his coins as testimony to his being a Buddhist.

In the seventh century, Xuanzang wrote that, during the winter, from the eastern Punjab, Kushan king Kanishka, grandson of Kadphises, took hostages from the neighboring territories of King Chinapati. The hostages brought with them Chinani peaches, which the local people called *China-rajaputra* (Chinese prince). The story is substantiated by Chinese peaches

The Great Stupa

still to be found in Jalandhar and Doab in the northwestern Punjab. Kanishka reigned in about the first century.

In 159162, after dream - ing of a man made of gold, the Chinese emperor Huan learned from his ministers of a person named Buddha (Fo in Chinese), who was worshipped in India. The emperor dispatched envoys to seek out the teachings of Fo.

During the Period of the Three Kingdoms (Wei, Wu, Shu; 220265), northwest India was part of Da Yuezhi territory for a while. During the Wei and Jin periods, relations between India and China were temporarily severed. The third-century kingdom of Funan, on the Mekong Delta, however, sent envoys to Pataliputra in India. Moreover, the emperor Taizong (93997) of the Song dynasty sent two envoys named Kangtai and Zhuying to Funan. In 502, the Gupta king sent envoys to China. The king, Narasimha-gupta, the successor of Buddha-gupta, sent the Indian monk Paramartha as envoy to the court of the Liang dynasty (502557) with a gift of a jade vessel.

In the seventh century, traffic between China and India became more frequent. A considerable number of records by travelers like Xuanzang, Wang Xuance, Yijing, and monks from China and the Korean kingdom of Silla whose names appear in Records of Distinguished Tang-Dynasty Priests Journeys to the West in Quest of the Dharma survive. According to research by Liang Qichao, the names of 169 such monks are known, although in actuality many times more probably set out for the western regions and India. It was safe for foreign priests to travel there in those days, when the central Asian lands along the Silk Road were politically and economically stable. In 638, a monk named Yuan Chan entered northwest India by way of Jalandhar in Afghanistan and spent four years at the Mahabodhi Temple. After returning home in 665, he traveled to India once again to make a pilgrimage to the Diamond Throne (Vajrasana) at Bodh Gaya. In 640, another monk named Hui Lun made the same pilgrimage.

As a bureaucrat and diplomatic envoy serving the Tang emperors Taizong and Gaozong, Wang Xuance, whose birth and death dates are uncertain, made three or four trips to India. Since he was a layman, his name does not appear in records of pilgrim priests. In addition to the Tang-dynasty Buddhist text *Fayuan zhulin*, numerous fragmentary records pertaining to him appear in *Jiu Tang shu* (Old Tang documents), *Xin Tang shu* (New Tang documents), the chronological and historical work called *Zizhi tongjian*, and the Song-dynasty encyclopedia *Cefu yuangui*. *Jiu Tang shu* states that he authored journals of his travels in India, including *Zhong Tianzhu xingji*, a 60-volume work on his travels westward, with 40 volumes of illustrations.

Recently more has been coming to light about Wang Xuance and his journeys. A fragment of his travel journal was discovered at Dunhuang and other pertinent records in the Tibetan Autonomous Region. Chinese scholars like Sun Canjuan have written on pertinent research published since 1932.

Many monks went to India in violation of governmental prohibitions. Unlike them, Wang Xuance was actually an official envoy of the Tang court. Although their names are unknown, in 641, numerous envoys came and went between China and Harshvardhan, king of Magadha, in central India. The *Fayuan zhulin* says that, on his first visit to India, Wang Xuance was an assistant. In March 643, the Tang emperor issued an edict to the effect that, in December of that same year, the envoy Li Yibiao and vice-envoy Wang Xuance accompany to the Indian kingdom of Magadha a certain Brahman then residing in China.

8 Chinese Imperial Envoy: Wang Xuance II

In 641, the Indian emperor Harshavardhana sent envoys and tribute to Tang-dynasty China. The Chinese emperor responded by dispatching to Harshavardhana Li Yibiao as chief envoy assisted. by Wang Xuance. He is said to have sent gifts of great pearls and to have ordered the building of a golden stupa beside the Bodhi Tree.

According to the *Xin Tang shu* (New Tang documents), in 648, at the death of Harshavardhana, a certain Arjuna assumed the royal title. On this occasion, with the assistance of Jiang Shihren and leading 1,200 Tibetan troops and 7,000 Nepalese groups, Wang Xuance defeated the city of Thanesar in three days, cutting off 3,000 heads, drowning 10,000, and taking 12,000 male and female prisoners, including members of the royal family. He is said to have captured 580 towns. For this exploit, Wang was made a Tang-court high military official. Other accounts further exaggerate it, but the event itself is surely factual. The Tang-dynasty Buddhist text *Fayuan zhulin* mentions Wang's having sent a Buddhist's priest's stole to India in 657.

He is said to have visited the room of Vimalakirti, the ideal lay believer of Buddhist tradition, in 660. The room, which was roughly 10 feet to a side and therefore *fangzhang* or approximately 100 feet squared, has given its name to temple abbots and to their quarters. Delighted by his visit, the local king entertained him with performing girls wielding three to 10 swords and magicians performing all kinds of magic. This seems to have been a country rich in colorful stories. The *Great Tang Records on the Western Regions* contains one tale relating how Shakyamuni convinced local fishermen not to try to kill a fabulous fish living in a nearby river. The creature had 18 heads, with two eyes apiece.

Datang xiyu qiufa gaoseng zhuan (*Records of Distinguished Tang-dynasty Priests' Journeys to the West in Quest of the Dharma*) describes how, as he was escorting the Brahman Lokayata back to China, Wang Xuance encountered a priest from Taizhou named Xuanzhao, who had been sent to India by the Tang emperor Gaozong in search of an elixir of eternal life and youth. The sought-for herb of immortality was said to be in a place called Luocha.

Owing to divergent opinions, it is not certain whether Wang Xuance traveled to India three or four times.

In 1990, at Gyirong in the Tibet Autonomous Region, a cliff-face stone inscription consisting of 24 lines of text was found. It mentions a Great Tang envoy to India and identifies a location of 82 degrees east longitude and 29 degrees north latitude. Though seriously damaged, the inscription is clearly legible. Apparently it memorializes a certain Wang Lingmin, from Xi, or modern Xi County in Henan, who accompanied Wang Xuance on this mission. Fragments of Wang Xuance's journal of his travels to India have been found at Dunhuang. The eight-line documents contain no personal names but mention a tower of King Ashoka and describe the place in detail, including the Buddha-footprint stone, monks, and the place where Shakyamuni carried out bodhisattva practices. (The material appeared in 2005 in *Dunhuang xuejikan*.)

Wang Xuance's name is recorded in Japanese history too. At the temple Yakushi-ji in Nara, a stone with Buddha footprints carved in the surface dates from 735. It is 69 centimeters

Buddha-footprints stone at the Yakushi-ji Temple in Nara (Photograph courtesy of the Yakushi-ji)

tall and 108 centimeters wide. The right foot is 47.7 centimeters from the tips of the toes to the heel; the left is 48.8 centimeters.

The stone carving was commissioned by the imperial prince Chino, later Fumiya no Chino. In addition to mentioning other stone carvings of Buddha footprints, it provides the information that the envoy of the Great Tang Wang Xuance traveled to Middle India and saw places associated with the Truth of Cause Effect like the Deer Park at Sarnath, where Shakyamuni preached his first sermonSet the Wheel of the Dharma in Motionand transcribed monuments.

Reverence for stone carvings of Buddha footprints originated in India and became popular in China and Japan. The presence in Japan of such a stone with a reference to the Tang envoy Wang Xuance is highly interesting.

9 Chinese Travel Journals: Xuanzang I

It is scarcely necessary to say that *Datang xiyu ji* (*Great Tang Records on the Western Regions*) by the Chinese monk Xuanzang Sanzang (c.600–64), who visited India in the seventh century, is the supreme source of information on the nature and state of Indian Buddhism 1,400 years ago. Indeed, the development of modern Indian archaeology today would be unthinkable without the material he provides. In producing his accurate accounts, however, he had the help of many collaborators including travel companions, controllers of the Silk Road, and state monarchs. Moreover, stable national conditions and economic prosperity were essential. In addition, many factors remain hidden and unmentioned in his records: horses to carry vast numbers of sutra scrolls, people to tend them, and expenses.

At a later age, Xuanzang's travel journal became the basis for the Chinese novel translated into English as *Journey to the West*. In it occur such fictional figures as the monkey Sun Wukong, who probably represent people who protected Xuanzang. Local gods encountered along the way and pilgrims descending from the sky to guard them from danger no doubt represent regional people who helped the party on its way.

Xuanzang was born around 600 (598 or 602 according to some accounts) during the Sui dynasty, as Chen Hui, in Guoshi near Luoyang in modern Henan Province. He was the fourth son of his father, Chen Hui (written with a different character), and his mother, Song Shi. Studying ancient scriptures at the age of eight, he had the reputation of being a child prodigy. Realizing that such study had to entail reading Sanskrit originals, he set his mind on making pilgrimages to the sacred Buddhist sites. In 629, violating the governmental prohibition by the then-ruling Tang dynasty against it, he left the country. With the aid of the king of Turpan Qu Wentai, he joined a group of merchants and, taking the northern route over the Tianshan Mountains, entered India from Gandhara and traveled extensively through various regions.

In giving information on places he did not actually visit himself, he reports "hearsay." In spite of a few errors in bearings, his reports of what he heard and saw are meticulous. At the university at Nalanda, he studied the Consciousness-only philosophy under Silabhadra, the head of the institution at the time. Xuanzang's visits to local Buddhist sites took place during the reign of King Harshavardhana. Returning with a cargo of 657 scriptural texts, he reached the Tang capital Chang'an in 645. Without referring to his criminal violation of the imperial ban on leaving the country, the emperor Taizong praised the achievements of Xuanzang, who finally died in 664 at the Yuhua Palace.

Having accepted the hospitality of King Harshavardhana, Xuangzang traveled down the Ganges to the metropolis of the kingdom of Magadha, Pataliputra, about the origin of the name of which he inquired. Proceeding southward, he turned toward Bodh Gaya along a highway passing through modern Jahanabad. From Gaya he climbed Mount Pragbodhi and, traveling four or five *li* (16–20 kilometers), arrived at the Bodhi Tree. Xuanzang describes Bodh Gaya and its environs in the following way.

The surrounding brick masonry railing is long north-south

Ananda, Ten Great Disciples of the Buddha **by Shiko Munakata (Collection of the Zojo-ji Temple)**

and short east-west. The circumferences is about 500 paces. There are unusual trees. Beautiful flowers are in bloom. Green plants of a kind I have never seen grow in the fine sand. On the eastthe frontit faces the Nairanjana River. On the south is a large flower pond. The west is enclosed by an embankment, and on the north is a path to a large monastery. The many stupas and temples inside the railing were built as memorials in homage to Shakyamunis teachings by Indian kings and ministers. Within the railing surrounding the Bodhi Tree is the *Vajrasana* or Diamond Throne, the stone on which Shakyamuni attained enlightenment. Its creation is coeval with that of the Earth; and of its foundation, only the top part, which is in the uppermost Golden Wheel of the world system, is visible. It is made of diamond and can be circumambulated in 100 paces. It is said that for ages as many as a thousand Buddhas have sat in meditation on this stone. Referred to as *Bodhi-manda*, the place under the Bhodi Tree where Shakyamuni attained enlightenment, it remains unmoving even should the earth itself shake.

Though it is said to have trembled when the enlightened Buddha walked around its four corners, it has not moved again since. In the world of the Latter Day of the Law, when the correct teaching can no longer be propagated, sand and earth will obscure it from sight. After Shakyamunis death, hearing of the size of the Diamond

Throne, monarchs of the lands erected two statues of the Bodhisattva Avalokiteshvara to demarcate its northern and southern boundaries. Old people say that when these bodhisattva figures are buried in dirt and invisible, the Buddha's teaching will fail. The statue on the south is already half buried.

In front of the Diamond Throne is the Bodhi Tree, a pipal tree. In the Buddha's lifetime, it was hundreds of feet tall but has gradually been cut back to only four or five feet. It is called the Bodhi Tree because Shakyamuni attained enlightenment (*bodhi*) while meditating under it.

10 Chinese Travel Journals: Xuanzang II

The Chinese monk-traveler Xuanzang (c.600–664) describes the Mahabodhi Temple of his time in the following way.

> East of the Bodhi Tree is a Monastery (the present Great Stupa), it is 160–70 feet tall and the base is about 20 paces in breadth. Built of blue bricks coated with plaster, it houses gilded statues on each level. The four walls are ornamented with rare gems and bear statues of heavenly immortals. At the pinnacle of the Great Stupa is a mango-shaped treasure vessel. On the east side is a pavilion with triple eaves, the posts, ridge posts, beams, and doors of which are ornamented with gold and silver carving set with pearls and jewels. The room is deep and has triple doors. On either side of the outer gate is a niche housing silver statues over ten feet tall. The one on the right represents Avalokiteshvara; and the one on the left, Maitreya. On the monastery grounds is a small temple first built by King Ashoka and later enlarged by a Brahman.

Xuanzang's description is accurate. The Nairanjana River still flows on the east of the site. There is a tank on the south side, and the monastery—though only its foundation—still exists on the north side. In the 1960s, the absence of railings around

Scroll 22 of the ***Five Hundred Buddha Disciples*** **by Kano Kazunobu (Collection of the Zojo-ji Temple)**

them gave visitors free access to the Diamond Throne (Vajrasana) and the Bodhi Tree. Now, however, they are surrounded by double and triple railings, over which the branches of the tree spread wide. In the 1960s, statues were to be seen only here and there in the Great Stupa niches. Today, all the niches enshrine figures of Buddhas and bodhisattvas.

The construction date of the Great Stupa, of which Faxian makes no mention, remains unknown. On the basis of examples from other parts of India, however, it seems likely that, as was true in these other instances, repeated expansions were made to an initially constructed small stupa. Xuanzang gives the date on which Shakyamuni attained enlightenment as the eighth day of the latter part of the Indian month Vaishaka, or the eighth day of the third month of the Chinese lunar calendar. The Buddha was 30 or 35 years old at the time.

Xuanzang visited a stupa erected to revere a place where the god Indra planted a stalk of grass as a temple and another to commemorate the important event when Shakyamuni resisted the Evil King and the wiles of the evil maidens who, after failing to seduce him, turned into hags. In his time, a stupa honoring the place where Indra requested the Buddha to share his teachings stood at the southeast corner of the railing around the Bodhi Tree. Within the monastery was a seated statue of the Buddha.

The tank where lived the Serpent King Mucalinda, who protected Shakyamuni physically from the wind and rain after he had attained enlightenment, was located in a grove on the east. Though blackish, its waters are described as beautiful. The place where Shakyamuni persevered in ascetic practices for six years is described as having been in a grove to the east of this tank. There is a statue of him in an emaciated condition after having survived on one sesame seed and one grain of wheat a day. Xuanzang makes simple mention of Shakyamuni's eating rice gruel but does not identify the person who gave it to him.

The story of the conversion of the three Kasyapa brothers, who had formerly been fire worshipers, and of the more than one thousand people converted with them is told in considerable detail.

Outside the north gate was the Great Mahabodhi Monastery commissioned originally by King Meghavana of Sri Lanka. It had six halls with three-story observation towers and housed a statue of the Buddha made of gold and silver and set with precious stones. A railing 40 or 50 feet high surrounded it.

The next pilgrim to visit India and leave a travel journal was Yijing (653–713) whose *Nanhai ji gui nei fa zhuan* (*Account of Buddhism Sent from the South Seas*) deals with the clothing, food, and housing of monks living a precepts-based monastic life at Nalanda, which he visited. His account has little to say, however, about historic sites and relics.

The *Datang xiyu qiufa gaoseng zhuan* (*Records of Distinguished Tang-Dynasty Priests' Journeys to the West in Quest of the Dharma*) interestingly lists 61 priests who traveled to Central India but only five who returned home safely. Forty of them went by sea route, whereas half returned by land and half by sea. Either way, they all had to be resigned to the mortal peril of the journey. The majority of the pilgrims were from China, though seven were from the Korean kingdom of Silla and others from Tokara and the Korean kingdom of Koguryo.

During the period between 627 and 649, one of these

monks, a man named Xuanzhao, from Xianzhang in Taizhou, studied Sanskrit with Xuanzheng of the temple Daxingsheng-si. After many hardships, he made a pilgrimage to the Great Stupa at Mahabodhi, where he remained for four years. He made several trips to India, visiting sites associated with the Buddha. It was he who, as has been said earlier, met Wang Xuance and accompanied him while he escorted the Brahman to Luocha in Western India in search of the herb that grants eternal life and youth. Xuanzhao died in India at the age of 60.

The empress Wu Zetian (625–705) had aided Yijing and, upon his return, welcomed him herself at the Upper Eastern Gate of the palace at Loyang.

11 Later Chinese Pilgrims

After the time of Yijing (653–713), Sino-Indian contacts diminished for a while; but during the Song dynasty (960–1279), the number of Chinese monks traveling to India grew. Characteristic of this period are large numbers of stone inscriptions left by these monks at the Bodh Gaya Great Stupa and surviving to the present. The English archaeologist Alexander Cunningham recorded them and published the original Chinese with English translations and commentaries by Samuel Beal in the *Journal of the Royal Asiatic Society*.

In one of the short inscriptions occurs a donor monk of the great Han dynasty (206 B.C.–220 A.D.) named Zhi-yi (Chi-I), who, when visiting the Great Stupa, requested that 300,000 people be reborn in heaven. To this end he made an offering of 300,000 sutras bearing his request. He and his companions traveled to many Buddhist sites, including Bodh Gaya in Magadha, where they worshipped at the Diamond Throne.

> Chi-I, a priest of the Great Han country having first vowed to exhort or encourage 30.000 men to prepare themselves by their conduct for a birth in heaven, to distribute in charity 30.000 books relating to a heavenly birth, himself to recite as many books, then, in company with others, travelled through India, and arrived at Maghada, where he

gazed upon the diamond throne and other sacred vestiges of his religion. After this, in company with some other priests, he further vowed to continue his travels through India apparently for the same purpose. Three of his companions were named Kwei-tseih, Chi-I, and Kwang-fung.

The three names found in the inscription bearing this information—Zhi-yi, Guangfeng (Kwang-fung), and Qingyun (Kwei-tseih)—are written in Han-dynasty characters. The inscription appears above depictions of Buddhas and the bodhisattva Maitreya but is unrelated to them. Much of the text has been effaced. Of course, "great Han" means China, and it is not surprising that a priest like Zhi-yi should wish for the birth in heaven of thousands of people. In this, he and his companions would have been similar. If it is correct to date it to the Han, this inscription must be one of the earliest. The next inscription to be discussed is so long that part of it has been omitted.

Record of a hymn of praise in honour of the body and throne of Buddha, by the Priest Ho-Yun, from the Western River of the Great Sun Empire, reciter of the Sutras.

I, Ho-Yun, having come from my far distant fatherland to gaze upon the territory of Buddha; and then having seen with my eyes the miraculous footprint, was I not respectfully to offer my homage in glorification of my God? I therefore collected together what of money I could spare, and some 30 paces to the north of the Bodhidruma I raised a stone to the Ten Thousand Buddhas.

On three occasions Chiang Hsia-pias spent here the season of fast; but he had not the wherewithal to express his deepfelt gratitude and overflowing respect, and was forced to content himself with eurogistic utterances upon the countenance of the birthless intelligence.

O great master, merciful to the people, sympathizing with all creatures, although you do not manifest yourself, still you are a most efficacious God. The herd of evil ones gaze up towards you and recognize your universal love increasing with the changing moons of the past two thousand years.

Oh, I could gaze on your lakshana for ever. The majesty of your countenance is rare indeed; the crown of your head is of fine serpentine; your eyes like lotus flowers in a pool; the svastika is written in gold upon your breast; the down of your shoulders is like threads of snow; wonderful indeed is your marvelous hand; the texture of your robes is impermeable to dust and smoke. And as Chiang Hsiapias had hymned the shadow, I determined to pronounce a eulogium on the body, of which Buddha has three in all. And I began with the Nirmana-kaya as follows; deep is your sympathy, genuine as the face of the moon; you have saved mortals from out of the midest of fire; your handsest down the traditions of the healing art; your stringest perals in branching relationships, The Three Vihicles lead the way to wisdom. The five precepts brush away confusing dust of the world; mental disturbance extinguishes the light of the intellect, but reaches not your body, which is beyond the pale of matter. I then proceeded to hymn the Sambhoga-kaya as follows; the myriad priests in the garden of Jeta, released from mortality, pass from the thraldom of desire, the dust of this earth is wiped away : they long to enter into possession of the middle kingdom. The body of every Buddha possesses illimitable potentialities; his heart is disserved from all ties: cast forever into the sea of Trilokya personal ambitions are entirely obliterated. To witness the source and wander over the sphere of the Law it was well to travel through dust and desert, bright, bright, without beginning or end; dark, dark, breaking the chain

Scroll 50 of the *Five Hundred Buddha Disciples* by Kano Kazunobu (Collection of the Zojo-ji Temple)

of nidana; dwelling on earth without becoming earthy: abiding in heaven without undergoing change; in this enlogium I utter the deepest words of my heart, for I have at length met with the Immaculate Body. And when I had eulogized the Triple Body, I desired also to eulogise the throne of each body, wherefore I proceeded to eulogise the shrine of Nirmana-kaya as follows: there are wondrous footprints in the Five Heavens, produced within the limits of the six cardinal points, in depth descending to the bottom of the golden chakra, in height reaching to the surface of the earth; never do any mortal cares mingle there, for how can fire and water blend ? Sometimes the army of maitreya and mara fight, until the latter are quelled by the roar of the lion. I then eulogized the shrine of Sambhoga-kaya, as follows: this shrine towers above the limits of the Tri-lokya; its shapely summit rests above the sky, the Kalpa of fire exercises no influence over it; on earth how should we seek to model its like? The reputation of King Ashoka extends afar: he rested in wonderful perception of the doctrine. A jewel among grains of sand, immortal, he will permeate the Great Void. I then eulogized of the shrine of the Dhrma-kaya, as follows: no beginning, no birth, no death; all distracting influences at the end; steadily pursuing the Five Gati; quietly entering into the kalpa of the Three Plagues. O supremest manifestation of wisdom, pure essence separated from the gross, even though passing through a hundred myriad kalpas, you would still be removed far from the dust of this earth. Thus with the most fitting of my poor language did I strive to glory the Great Doctrine, measuring, as it were, with the eye of a mosquito, the vast expanse of sky, perceiving not the magnitude of my task, but anxious only to give expression to my heart's burden. And now I take these hymns on the Triple Body, consummate in its excellence, and cause them to be engraved, in the hope that prosperity and long life may thereby accrue to my honored Prince, the Sovereign of the Great Sung Empire. For His majesty is humbly desirous that the destiny of the Doctrine may resemble that of the Sacred Pool, from which nothing may be taken, and to which nothing may be added, the wave of which are liable neither to increase nor decrease; its blessedness that of the Celestial Hill, enduring in majestic loftiness. Still more does my Prince desire that in the future of this kingdom shrine may be added to shrine, and that in other land and other ages name upon name may be enrolled among the legions of the faithful. Also that others may hymn the praise of the miraculous footprint, and cause the same to be similarly voted down and put on record.

Recorded, and set up in token thereof, this Jen-hsu year of the regn of Divine, Favour of the Great Sung Empire (A.D. 1021)

In postscript the priest Yun-shu adds the following: There went with me to worship in the land of Buddha the two priests I-ching and I-lin,from the monastery of Established Doctrine in the High Street of the Eastern Capital, who each took with him a gold embroidered Kashaya to be hung up in the shrine of Mahabodhi, and each set up his own own memorial tablet in perpetual remembrance thereof.

The priest Ke-yun (Ho-Yun) from the West River traveled far to revere the Diamond Throne at Bodh Gaya. Thirty paces north of the place of enlightenment (Bodhimanda), he erected a stone stupa in honor of the Thousand Buddhas. The text offers praise to the Three Bodies of the Buddha; that is, according to Mahayana Buddhism, the Dharma or True Body, which represents the teachings; the Incarnation Body, which manifests itself in this world; and the Reward Body created through discipline in the way of the bodhisattva, like that of the Buddha Amitabha. One of the rare examples relating Buddhist teachings, this inscription is especially valuable. It goes on to pray for the long life of the Song-dynasty emperor. The inscription was carved by two monks Yi-qing (I-ching) and Yi-lin (I-lin) from the "Monastery of Established Doctrine in the High Street of the Eastern Capital," who also hung a gold-brocade priest's stole on the Bodhi Tree.

12 The Travel Journal of Dharmasvamin

In the 12th century, as Islamic incursions grew more violent, India fell into a state of political and social insecurity. Fear of mortal danger drastically reduced the number of travelers in the region. Nonetheless, even under such circumstances, one Tibetan monk visited central India to tour the Buddhist sacred sites. His name was Chak-Lotsa-wa (1197–1263 or 64), though he is better known as Dharmasvamin. His account of his journey is our only key to knowledge of conditions prevailing in India in the mid-13th century. His lifetime overlaps roughly with that of Honen Shonin (1133–1212) in Japan.

Probably born in 1197, Dharmasvamin traveled in India between 1234 and 1236, at a time when practically no copies of Buddhist scriptures survived there. All he was able to garner were a few works picked up at Nalanda and Bodh Gaya. His uncle Dharmasvamin the Elder had traveled to India and died there.

For 22 years prior to 1226, Dharmasvamin received primary and middle education and studied grammar, logic, philosophy, higher philosophy (*abhidharma*), Yoga, and Guhyasamaja Tantra. In addition, he became well versed in mantra drawing, medicine, sculpture, and painting and wrote a book on the fourth-century poet Kalidasa.

First he entered Nepal and, under Ratnaraksita and Rabindra, studied Tantra and spells at the Swayambhu Chaitya stupa and the Dharmadatu Vihara, located near the national border. In 1234, when he was 37, he decided to move on to India, which was so dangerous at the time that his associates tried to dissuade him. But for him the distances involved were shorter than they had been for the Chinese monks since the fifth century, and no emigration or immigrations restrictions were in effect. Moreover language study was easy for him, and probably a large number of ordinary Nepalese lived there. No record of his having organized a sizeable caravan survives.

Setting out alone for India in the spring of 1234, he spent three months reaching Tirhut. Then, to avoid Muslim troops, he spent 17 days more before reaching central India. He passed his first rainy-season retreat at Bodh Gaya from July to October of the same year.

The following year he visited Gridhrakuta and Rajagriha and studied with Mahapandita Yasomitra. From January to April 1235, at Nalanda, he studied Sanskrit grammar with Rahula Shribhadra, who, then 90 years old, had 70 disciples and, knowledgeable in Tibetan, helped translate the *Kalachakravatia* into that language. He urged Dharmasvamin to return home because, the preceding year, a Tibetan monk at Nalanda had contracted a high fever and died. As his teacher had feared, Dharmasvamin did fall ill but, after suffering a fever and a rash, recovered and ended his two-year stay in March 1236.

Setting out in June, he reached Tibet either at the end of that same year or the beginning of 1237. Staying at the Yandog monastery near the border, he compiled a commentary on the *Namasangiti* and collected numerous manuscripts. When he left, he had with him 150 volumes of sutras plus six copies of the *Pancavimsatisahasrika-prajnaparamita-sutra* (*25,000-Line Perfection of Wisdom Sutra*) and two copies of the *Astasahasrika-prajnaparamita-sutra* (*8,000-Line Perfection of Wisdom Sutra*). In addition, he carried back to his own monastery

Tibetan monks

from Yan-dog such things as dyes and sugar.

A noteworthy account claims that, at one point during the 23 years Dharmasvamin spent at his home monastery, the Yuan emperor of China Kublai Khan (121594) sent an envoy inviting him to visit. The invitation was refused. Although Dharmasvmins dates do not correspond with those of the reign of Kublai Khan, the story nonetheless suggests the extent to which the Tibetan pilgrims fame had spread. In 1263, Dharmasvamin gave all his property to charity. He died at the age of 68 on Wednesday, the 10th day of the half of the bright month Margasirsha of the year Wood-Male-Mouse (January 1264). It is said that, at his passing, rainbows appeared in the sky, which rained down celestial flowers.

Dharmasvamin said in his records that the Bodhisattva Avalokiteshvara constantly protected him throughout the many perils he encountered in India. Belief in this bodhisattva has persisted down the ages, as is indicated by the modern-day chanting of the Avalokiteshvara mantra: *Om manipadme hum.*

In speaking of the Diamond Throne (Vajrasana), Dharmasvamin wrote, Southwards from the border of Vaisali, at a distance of eight stages, lies Vajrasana. There is also the river Ganga. The river flows from west to east. Having started early in the morning, one did not reach (the opposite bank of the river?) till evening. At the time of the visit to Vajrasana, the place was deserted and only four monks were found staying (in the Vihara).... They blocked up the door in front of the Mahabodhi image with bricks and plastered it...on its surface they drew the image of Mahesvara in order to protect it from non-Buddhists.... At daybreak they fled towards the North... and for 17 days the face of the image (i.e. the Mahabodhi image) was not to be seen. One day we heard that the Muslim soldiers had gone far away.... The Raja came riding out of the forest on an elephant." The reverence the Raja paid to Dharmasvamin is described in detail.

This account suggests that, instead of remaining in one place, Muslim troops could visit various sacred Buddhist sites.

Like Xuanzang, Dharmasvamin describes the vicinity of the Great Stupa in detail, mentioning the Gandhola (fragrant abode) built by the king Ashoka, the Tathagata's tooth, the stone railing erected by Nagarjuna, and the small shrine to the goddess Tara. He refers to the so-called conch shell blown by Nagarjuna, a hole the size of a human head in a clay wall. A person who placed his ear at that hole at sunrise was said to hear sounds presaging the arrival of summer. He also describes the place under the Bodhi Tree where Shakyamuni sat meditating on a mat made of *kusa* grass.

13 Bodh Gaya under the Mahants

With Muslim incursions and the dispersal of Buddhist believers, the Mahabodhi Temple fell into ruins not to appear in history again until 1590, when a Shaïvite monk named Gossain Ghamandi Giri, an heir to the tradition of the eighth-century philosopher Shankara, visited it while on a pilgrimage. Struck by its tranquility, he built a retreat in which to take up his residence. Thereafter, up to 1802, 12 generations of successive Hindu abbots, or mahants, called themselves *giri*, although their full names and dates differ from record to record. In the 21st century, regulations stipulate that one of the nine members of the Bodh Gaya Temple Management Committee shall bear the *giri* title. As late as 2008, that member was Mahant Sri Sudarshan Giri.

A man of great learning and virtue, the second mahant, who assumed his post in 1615, Chaitanya Giri was well loved by all. His successor, Mahadeva Giri, built a small shrine to the goddess Annapurna provider of a vessel that always pours forth boundless grain. (The vessel is said still to be in the temple's possession.) Chaitanya Giri is attributed with erecting a spacious mahant monastery, or *math*, beside the Falgu River. The Mogul emperor in Delhi conferred on Lal Giri, who assumed office in 1682, six manors including the Taradih, mentioned earlier in this series. Later bearers of the *giri* title were to acquire more manors and increasing wealth.

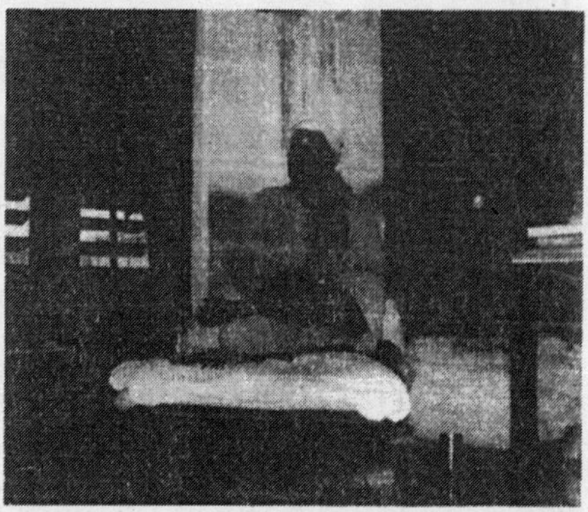
Mahant Sudarshan Giri

In 1819, the British government recognized the office of Mahant of Bodh Gaya. In 1840, the *giri* aided British troops in dealing with the Sepoy rebellion known as the Indian Mutiny. A great Sanskrit scholar and collector of numerous manuscripts, Hemu Narayan Giri, the eleventh holder of the title, established a library for his extensive collection of manuscripts, created an institution in Varanasi to care for elderly priests, opened numerous pilgrims lodgings, and conducted excavations of ruins. He planned many expedient policies to aid the government during the famine of 1773. Even today, descendants of people he benefited are said to revere him highly. On January 1, 1877, Queen Victoria bestowed a title on him. In 1887, his successor, Krishna Dayal Giri, spent 2,500 rupees in the currency of the time on repairs to the Mahabodhi Temple.

A mahant must be single and is chosen by five members of a council, none of whom may be nominated mahants. Election must be unanimous. Funds from alms, manor income, and personal income are used for periodic dinners and occasional festivals, limited to Hindu festivals like Dusshehra. Considerable money is spent on ceremonies to inaugurate a new mahant upon the death of another, when large quantities of a sweet called *malpua* are served. Financial power is put to use in investments and the acquisition of foreign stocks and real estate. Everyone from grass cutters to high-ranking priests and manor managers is regarded as a disciple of the Shaivite Mahant. During the 1800s, Krishna Dayal Giri, a devout person and an ardent businessman, donated 5,000 rupees to the G. A. Grierson

Endowment.

The above information comes from *A Brief History of Bodh Gaya Math* written by Narayan Singh Bahadur on orders from the governor of Gaya in 1892. An appendix to this book is of interest. One after another of the Mughal emperors of India granted royal warrants to the owners of the land on which Bodh Gaya stands. These documents later posed a supreme problem for the movement to return Bodh Gaya to Buddhist hands. They were issued with nine seals and the names and dates of granting emperors. But given in a Mughal or a local reckoning, the dates are sometimes difficult to convert to the Western calendar.

In addition to the seal, the content of the grant is set forth in detail including dates and manor areas. In the 18th century, signatures of British rulers of India appear on such documents. All of them recognize Bodh Gaya as the property of the mahants and include registration numbers, district names, personal names, approval dates, recorded areas, actual areas, and dates on which the grants were issued. Seventeen of these documents, all bearing seals, have been found. One of them contains information on arms possession issued by the police in 1881.

A final list of 212 (or 116) manors giving province, district name, real estate name, annual income, and prices makes it perfectly clear that in the 19th century, Bodh Gaya was legally and completely incorporated in the structure of British rule. Supported by immense wealth and authority, while behaving like state monarchs, bearers of the *giri* title protected the population.

Rising above the banks of the Falgu River, the present mahant math has tens of rooms and a farm on the grounds. People pray at its numerous Hindu shrines. Living on the topmost story, the mahant can look down on numerous domestic and foreign visitors observing the throne and its tiger skin (complete with head) and portraits and photographs of successive mahants. The high-ceilinged gate recalls the numbers of elephants that once came and went but now are no more. Nor is there any trace of the many Buddhist statues brought from the Great Stupa. The stupa itself, however, with its bustling shops is still visible from the rooftop.

14 The Hardships of Dharmapala

As is seen in the preceding discussion, non-Buddhist abbots, called mahants, came to reside at the semi-ruined Mahabodhi Temple at Bodh Gaya. It is not true, however, that Buddhists completely stopped frequenting the temple. Embassies and pilgrims, including members of the royal family, continued to arrive from Burma (Myanmar). Under British rule, it was easy to come and go in Burma, India, and Pakistan as if in a single country. One devout Buddhist named Don David Hewavitarane (later called Anagarika Dharmapala; 1864–1933) from Ceylon (Sri Lanka) made a pilgrimage to the Mahabodhi Temple on January 20, 1891. Concerned about its condition, he decided to restore the temple and, establishing the Mahabodhi Society in Colombo that same year, initiated a movement to return the sacred place to Buddhist hands. But things did not go as he intended.

A trial was held in the Calcutta High Court in August 1895, William Mac Pherson and Gurudas Banderjee presiding, relative to an incident that had occurred at the Mahabodhi Temple on January 1 of the same year. The text of the court's decision outlines the case as follows. Although the main text is concise, legal terminology and a special style make the part setting forth reasons difficult to understand. By the time of this trial, under section 296 of the Indian Penal Code, a regional lower court had already sentenced the injuring parties—the mahant of Bodh Gaya and his associates—to one month penal servitude and a fine of 100 rupees. In the trial under discussion, the mahant is appealing this sentence.

The lower court stated that "... about one-third of the human race, (regards the Mahabodhi Temple) as the most sacred spot on earth," and that for this reason the case is of great importance. As defendant, the mahant argued that this assertion was mistaken and that the matter was a regional one.

The following description of the incident is given. Between eight and nine on the morning of January 25, 1825, Dharmapala, a Buddhist from Ceylon and the honorary general secretary of the Mahabodhi Society, in the company of two Singhalese Buddhist priests, Sumangala and Devananda, and a layman, Silva, of the same race and religion were installing a statue of Buddha, sent from a temple (Tentoku-ji Temple*) in Japan on the second floor of the Mahabodhi Temple. At the time, the special sub-registrar and deputy magistrate of Gaya (both Muslims) happened to be present, as did the Muslim Hussain Baksh, the mahant's steward, and Jagannat Singh, a Hindu doorkeeper kept at the temple by the mahant. All of these parties departed before the statue was enshrined.

After everything, including candles and lotus blossoms were in place, Dharmapala reported the fact to the government custodian of the temple. Six or seven minutes later, when Sumangala was about to light the candles, 30 or 40 Hindu priests and Hussain Baksh forced their way into the room. Blocking Dharmapala, some of them snatched away the candle Sumangala held, thus preventing his lighting the others. Claiming to have 500 followers, the intruders told Dharmapala that, unless he destroyed it, they would toss the Buddha statue out. Baksh shoved Dharmapala hard in the back as he ordered him to take the statue away. The government custodian tried to halt the proceedings but, because of linguistic difficulties,

The Gandhakuti (Hall of Fragrance) established by Dharmapala in Sarnath

failed.

A certain Vijayananda happened to be present on some official business at the time. Once Dharmapala had explained the situation to him, the intruders left. Thinking opposition action had ceased, Dharmapala and the two priests took their places beside the statue. But, about 15 minutes later, the Hindus returned and threw the statue out. Shortly thereafter, a constable and the head constable arrived and attempted to convince Hussain Baksh but to no avail. It should be said that Dharmapala seems not to have informed supervisory personnel in advance about his intention of enshrining the statue.

It was in connection with these events that Dharmapala made accusations resulting in the first-trial decision noted above. The sentences were reversed, however, by the second trial before the Calcutta High Court. The reversal was made on the grounds that interference had been limited and did not amount to obstruction of religious worship and ceremonial as stipulated in criminal law. Consequently, since section 296 of the Indian Penal Code did not apply in this instance, fines were returned. Dharmapalas evidence was criticized and his efforts cited as causes for the fruitlessly lengthy duration of court proceedings.

Ostensibly, this decision indicated that liberty to visit the Mahabodhi Temple by people of any and all faiths was not interfered with. But it was also a decision implying the need for cooperation on the part of Hindus, who, under British colonial control, constituted 80 percent of the population of India.

The trial, in which the viceroy Lord Curzon (1859–1925) took an interest, produced an immense record of opinions on issues related to Indian archaeology.

In an article published in 1999, Nayanjoy Lahiri, a professor in the History Department of Delhi University, vigorously rejected the idea that believers in other faiths had been hindered from visiting the Mahabodhi Temple. She attributes the occurrence of other conflicts in the 19th century to the rise of Tantric Buddhism under the influence Hindu Tantric doctrines and a reappraisal of Buddhism in the West on the part of missionaries in colonial India. These factors accelerated a Buddhist revival movement. Furthermore, advances in communications methods promoted the internationalization of Buddhism, as improved transportation systems facilitated pilgrim travel. Indeed, these factors were to relate to the numerous trips Dharmapala made to Japan in search of support and the receipt of the Buddha statue from the Tentoku-ji Temple.

Many of the articles in the 2012 collection of the latest research on Mahabodhi support the opinion that the temple is pan-religious in nature.

*The Tentoku-ji Temple belongs to the Jodo-shu Tokyo Parish Jonan Group. The statue in question represents the Buddha Amitaba (Amida) and is presently enshrined, in its still damaged condition, at the Mahabodhi Association in Kolkata (Calcutta).

15 The Travel Journal of Francis Buchanan Hamilton

Starting in the 18th century, when the British ruled the country, large numbers of English people lived for extended periods in India. Aside from Francis Buchanan Hamilton, however, few left written accounts of their travels there. Born in Scotland, Hamilton was a physician who had detailed knowledge of geography, zoology, biology, and mineralogy too. He wrote accounts of his travels in southern India in *A Journey from Madras through the Countries of Mysore, Canara and Malabar* (1807). He also wrote *An Account of the Kingdom of Nepal* (1819), and especially exhaustive accounts of conditions in northern India in his journal on Bihar, Patna, and Gaya (1925 edition).

These records are richly illustrated with maps (though place names are often given in Persian forms) and detailed information on flora and fauna. Between 1794 and 1815, he traveled throughout Bengal and the administrative district of the East India Company, keeping records of his travels. All of his manuscripts were left to the British Library and published later as the centrally important *Bihar and Patna* (3 volumes), and *Patna and Gaya* (1811–12). In the former, he sets forth with absolute reliability and accuracy local topographical features like mountains, rivers, and lakes; natural resources (minerals); climate; ancient sites and remains; ethnic groups; agriculture (rice, wheat, other cereals, vegetables, sugar, rapeseed, tobacco, dyes, and indigo); domestic animals (cattle, pigs, and chickens); commerce (salt trade, markets, and merchants); statistics; and weights and measures.

The account of his trip to Bodh Gaya begins on October 16, 1811, when he moved from Monghir to Surajgarh. On October 18, his road took him southward along the Ganges to Balgudar. Walking westward to Patna on November 4, then farther west to the Sone River then south, he reached Jehenabad on the 13th and the Barabar caves on the 21st. On November 26, he reached Sahebganji (Gaya) and from the 29th climbed Ram Sil hill and Preth Sila hill, both Hindu sacred places. Of Gaya he wrote, "The streets are narrow (6 to 10 feet) dirty and crooked.... The very best houses are rendered slovenly by cakes of cowdung for fuel patched on their walls.... None of the Gyalis would have communication with me...I was accompanied by the most learned *sanyasi* (ascetic) of Buddh Gaya."

The gods Ganesha, Narayana, and Kali were worshipped everywhere. He visited the Vishnupad Temple, whose builders he could not name. Some Sanskrit inscriptions in the town dated to 1277 (Vikram calendar). He then visited Brahma Yoni hill, his description corresponds exactly with the place as it is today. On December 9, 1811, he visited the mahant's math, or Hindu monastery, (owner of the Great Stupa at the time) six miles down the Falgu River. The mahant, or abbot, at the time was named Soruju Giri. Most of the building materials for the monastery were obtained from ruins. Some inscriptions were in Burmese characters. There were many Buddhist statues. After crossing the Niranjana River eastward, he climbed Pragbodhi hill.

On one occasion, what he thought was only a hill turned out to be a ruined temple made of brick and earth. People remember it as the Mahamuni Temple. When building a house of bricks there, a certain Englishman named Charles Boddam removed from a hole a stone box containing human bones and a

The Great Stupa before reconstruction

statue of a god. A stone pillar that was there had been carried off to the town of Gaya. A large statue of Bhairava was found there too. All of these comments are interesting indications of what the place was like in Buchanan Hamiltons time.

Of the Great Stupa he wrote to the following effect. There is a tank on the south side of the stupa; the Bodhi Tree is on the west. The stupa is a quadrangular pyramid on a square base 2030 feet (3248 meters) high. Apart from the ornamentation, it is of plastered brick with niches presumably intended to house Buddhist statuary. Except on the north and west, damage is extensive. On the west is a tree allegedly planted by King Ashoka but probably no more than about 100 years old. There are doors on three sides of the main tower, around which are smaller stupas. A Buddha statue is enshrined in the very small inner room. Deep inside the room is a lion throne before which is a clay statue of Shakyamuni. The mahant was said recently to have had repairs carried out on the staircase leading to the second story, but Muslims had carried away numerous Buddha statues. Although no plans of the stupa survive, photographs taken by Cunningham while excavating indicate that Buchanan Hamiltons descriptions are accurate. Though originally inside the building, the Lion Throne has been moved to a position next to the Bodhi tree.

Returning to Gaya on December 10, Buchanan Hamilton makes several comments on the temperature, which remained at about 106 degrees F. Thereafter moving northeast, he visited Rajagriha on January 18, 1812, spending his time in a fulfilling way by investigating the hill minerals as he visited many historical sites on January 19 before departing on the 20th. He rode an elephant. Explanation of the castle itself—said to have been built by Sheer Shah—caused him to think of the Buddha and of Mahavira, founder of Jainism. The Cavern of Indra, where the Buddha is said to have delivered sermons, is located north of the castle. There are five hot springs in the vicinity; Buchanan Hamilton mentions their temperatures. He comments on Jain women who, as was unusual in India, bathed there naked. He mentions frogs in the paddy fields and comments on Buddhist or Jainist figures holding lotus blossoms and seated on Lion Thrones depicted on other hot-springs walls and on four Buddhist statues on the walls of another hot spring. He says nothing of Nalanda, probably because it was in a ruined state.

16 Doryu Kitabatake, a Japanese Pilgrim

The first Japanese to aspire to go to India was Prince Takaoka, the third son of the emperor Heizei (773–824). After abandoning secular life for the life of religion and changing his name to Shinnyo, he departed the port at Dazaifu (government headquarters on Kyushu) in 862, bound for Mingzhou (modern Ninbo) and arrived in Chang'an in 864. The following year, he set sail from Guangzhou headed for India but disappeared somewhere on the Malay Peninsula. In 882, a visiting student in Tang China voiced it abroad that a tiger had eaten him. (Incidentally, the prince was the uncle of the aristocratic poet Ariwara no Narihira.)

India-ink documents relating 14 cases of Japanese pilgrims to Angkor Wat in Cambodia between 1612 and 1632 have been found. Although the exact dates of the document for 1632 are uncertain, it is in the handwriting of one Morimoto Ukondayu Kazufusa, who traveled to this site on a ship belonging to the Kyushu Matsuura Clan. The museum known as the Mito Shokokan, in Mito, Ibaraki Prefecture, owns a plan drawing of Angkor Wat labeled, the Jetavana Monastery, no doubt by someone who really believed it represents the pageantry of the famous Buddhist site, which is actually located in Saheth Maheth in northern India.

Still later, Doryu Kitabatake (1820–1907), who led a turbulent life, traveled to India and left his own travel journal,

Tenjuku Koroji Shoken (Observations on the path to India). Born at a temple called the Hofuku-ji, in what is now Wakayama Prefecture, he studied the Confucianism of Ogyu Sorai (1666–1728), Chinese literature, and the Buddhist scriptures as well as the use of such weapons as rifle, sword, and lance. He argued that Buddhist priests should be returned to secular life and take part in developing the northern Japanese island Hokkaido.

When the Tokugawa shogunate ordered the Kishu Clan to calm a certain disorder, he led 250 soldiers who were secularized priests and, pitching camp on Mount Koya, resoundingly defeated the enemy. Later he set up a private school at Yurakucho in Tokyo. In 1882, during the Satsuma Rebellion (Seinan War) in opposition to the restored imperial government, he traveled to Tabaruzaka, on Kyushu to conduct memorial services including chanted prayers to the Buddha Amida (*nembutsu*) for many of the war dead. He then he planned an undertaking together with the statesman Munemitsu Mutsu (1844–97), but it fell through.

He traveled extensively in Europe. Wishing to visit Shakyamuni's tomb in India, in the winter of 1881, he sailed from Yokohama first for Marseilles. Thereafter he traveled to the United States before returning to Europe and finally making a pilgrimage to Bodh Gaya. On January 24, 1884, he arrived back in Yokohama, where he was greeted by the priest Mokurai Shimaji, Munemitsu Mutsu, Tokan Kizo (Tada), and Seiran Ouchi. The expenses of his travels were defrayed by the temple Hongan-ji. In May 1885, Kitabatake received 886 votes in the campaign sponsored by the *Konnichi Shimbun* newspaper to select the ten most popular people in the country.

With a knowledge of the German language, Kitabatake traveled through the West meeting many famous people and exchanging ideas on a wide range of topics including politics, economics, history, and religion. Though the transliterations he used in his writings in representing non-Japanese words were correct in their day, some of them are impossible to decipher now.

His European tour started in Paris. He discussed with Hermann Oldenberg the theory of transmigration, the Buddhist scriptures and non-Buddhist writings in in Berlin. In Germany, Otto von Bismarck's power and martial might astounded him. He spoke of the educational system and, while mentioning its three religions—Roman Catholicism, Protestantism, and Judaism—considered all Germany as one kingdom. In England he met up with a compatriot named Yuji Kurosaki from Ibaraki Prefecture. Having become traveling companions, the two embarked from Liverpool on the perilous voyage among the icebergs to America. Arriving in New York in early May 1883, they commented on numerous immigrants—two or three thousand—from Europe. At the time, it had become possible to cross from New York to San Francisco by train in a mere seven days and seven nights. Kitabatake said with admiration that the railroad must have been made by the hand of God. In Washington, D.C., they both felt the greatness of George Washington and came into contact with Mormonism.

After further journeying back to England and in the countries of Northern Europe, on October 15, 1883; they set sail from England and landed in Bombay on November 15. Following information provided by a Mr. Banerjee, he set out for Bodh Gaya. They arrived there at a time when about 120 people were in the midst of excavations. In reply to his inquiry about the nature of their work, they told him they were excavating the tomb of Shakyamuni. Descending 45 stone steps into the excavation, he encountered the excavation supervisor, who turned out to speak English.

"When I heard that this was the great tomb of Shakyamuni, I hurried madly down the stone steps and, without thinking, bounded and threw my arms around Kurosaki, exclaiming that this was the tomb of the Righteous Shakyamuni. Jumping for delight and joy, unable to stop, I ran around my compatriot, no doubt producing a strange impression.

Kitabatake expressed this experience in a *tanka* (a verse form that in Japanese has 31 syllables).

> Gaya village, now a mere name, is where I trace the Buddha today.

Master Doryu Kitabatake

To the right of the Great Stupa at the Mahabodhi Temple Kitabatake erected a stone monument on which was written in Japanese the information that this marked the first Japanese pilgrimage to the tomb of Shakyamuni since the beginnings of Japan. It was dated December 4, 1883 (16th year of the Meiji era). The monument can be seen in a photograph of Shoyu Hanayama and others taken in 1956. Now, however, no one knows what has happened to it. Nonetheless references to it in Kitabatakes writings and in many other books make it clear that it did indeed once exist. It is said that two stone fragments forwarded by a certain Dak Bengomentioned to Kitabatake by the excava - tion supervisor at Bodh Gayafound their way home by way of Kolkata.

17 From the Bodh Gaya Temple Act of 1949 to the Present

In spite of Dharmapala's efforts, restoring the Mahabodhi Temple to Buddhist hands proved difficult. For one thing, Dharmapala was not an Indian by nationality and did not conduct priest education. The Maha Bodhi Society, which he founded, stopped participating in site restorations by the Archaeological Survey of India and the building of new temples by various governments and is now limited to temples of Sri Lankan priests.

When the general meeting of the Indian National Congress party on February 16, 1922, officially took up the issue of the Mahabodhi Temple, negotiations between the Hindu mahants and the Buddhists shifted into the field of politics. At another general conference in 1924, the National Congress approved the formation of a committee under the leadership of Rajendra Prasad, who was later to become president of India, to deliberate rights of ownership and supervision. Although the committee drew up a draft of the Bodh Gaya Act, it was not put into effect. A later private Burmese proposal, too, produced no solution. It was not till June 19, 1949, after Indian independence had been achieved, that the Bodh Gaya Act was finally passed by the government of the state of Bihar. On April 26, 1953, the committee met for the first time; and on May 29, 1953, at 5:30 in the afternoon, transferal ceremonies from the mahant to the supervisory committee were held.

Provisions were made for a committee consisting of four Buddhists and four Hindus with the district magistrate of Gaya as ex-officio chairman. This meant the chairman would inevitably be Hindu, though all committee members were Indian citizens. Then, in November 1959, with the enactment of the Bodh Gaya Temple Advisory Board Act, provisions were revised to call for a purely advisory body of 20 members, two-thirds of whom must be Buddhists.

The supervisory committee has the following duties:

- Maintenance and repairs.
- Use of temple lands.
- Welfare of pilgrims.
- Appropriate conducting of worship at the temple and of *pindadana* offerings on temple lands.
- Prevention of desecration of revered images at the temple or any part thereof.
- Receipt and disposition of offerings at the temple.
- Sure safekeeping of financial statements and any other records concerning the temple and of all temple property.
- Safekeeping of all temple funds and arrangements for all temple savings and investments.
- Provisions for appropriate remuneration to salaried temple employees.

At present, in spite of valid ordinances, the state government has the ultimate deciding voice in all disputes arising between Hindus and Buddhists in connection with the temple and use of temple lands.

The committee has no jurisdiction over the property of the Shaivite temple. Regardless of this law or all provisions included in it or in any regulations based on it, the committee has no jurisdiction over movables located at Bodh Gaya that are the property of the Shaivite temple.

The first chairman of the supervisory committee was K. N. Singha, assistant district magistrate, Bodh Gaya. The director-general was Kishore Pandit Singh, member of parliament.

In 2009, the committee members were as follows:

Chairman: S. K. Singh
Chief Monk: Bhikkhu Chalinda
Members: Nangzey Dorjee, N. S. Sasai, Mahant Sudarshan Giri, Gyaneshwar Mahathera, M. Maharathi, K. Verma, R. Mishra, A.K. Singh

The advisory board has 25 appointed members, including an ambassador from Japan.

Established in Japan in 1968 thanks to the devoted efforts of Iwaya Shonin of the Jodo temple Yuten-ji, the International Buddhist Brotherhood Association has engaged in numerous activities at Bodh Gaya. In 1973, the International Buddhist Center and the Indosan Nippon Japanese Temple were completed. The first International Buddhists Rally was held in 1976. In 1977, the free-of-charge nursery school called the Bodaiju Gakuen was opened; a free-of-charge clinic began operation in 1984. In 2008, with many high-ranking Indian government officials in attendance, ground-breaking ceremonies were held for the Buddhism and Oriental Philosophy Research Institute. Affiliated with the Indosan Nippon Japanese Temple, the institute is a joint endeavor of the International Buddhist Brotherhood Association and the World Fellowship of Buddhists.

In 2002, the Mahabodhi Temple became a designated World Heritage site (historical architecture), and extensive development plans were proposed.

Appendix 1

Sanad granted under the seal of His Majesty Muhammad Sháh Pádsháh Gázi.

Muhammad Sháh Pádsháh Gázi. Era 8th Muhammad Sháhi. Seal of Nasrát Jang Itmádu'd-daulah Wazir al Mumálik Qamaru'd-din Khán, Khán Bahádur.	Seal of Muhammad Sháh Pádsháh Gázi. (In Togra character.)

Be it known to all present and future gumáshtas and mutsaddís of pargana Sherghâti, Sarkár and Súbá Bihár, that according to the order of His Majesty the King of all lands and time, Khalífá of strict justice and means of preservation and comfort to all beings (may God preserve him), who is the minister of the God of Gods, on whom is the special mercy of the Almighty Father, and who is the sole means of livelihood to the whole world, the root of all laws and regulations, and the preserver of the throne of the *khalafat*, written on the 21st day of Ziqád in the 9th year of his Jalus (accession), mauza Bagulá and Dharahrá khurd, are granted to Lál Gir Sannyási as *madad másh*, without any restriction of names and divisions from the middle of *bijiail*. You all, in obedience to this order, should leave the said mauzas in his possession, without making any change or alteration therein, and you should in no way be overcome by any kind of temptation, and should in all respect look upon the order as just and right, so that all the produce of the said property be used by him for his own livelihood and that of the itinerant faqirs; for which act of benevolence, he should ever pray for the stability of the wealth (of His Majesty). You all should not take notice of other properties belonging to the grantee. You all should take great care in carrying out this order.

Written this day, the 1st day of Rabiulawal in the 9th year of the August Jalús (accession).

Sanad granted under the seal of His Majesty Muhammad Sháh Pádsháh Gázi.

Muhammad Sháh Pádsháh Gázi. Era 8th Muhammad Sháhi. Seal of Nasrát Jang Itmádu'd-daulah Wazir al Mumálik Qamaru'd-din Khán, Khán Bahádur.	Seal of Muhammad Sháh Pádsháh Gázi. (In Togra character.)

Be it known to all present and future gumáshtas and mutsaddís of pargana Mahar, Sarkár and Súbá Bihár, that according to the order of His Majesty the King of all lands and time, and Khalífa of strict justice and means of preservation and comfort to all beings (may God preserve him), who is the minister of the God of Gods, on whom is the special mercy of the Almighty Father, who is the root of all the laws and regulations of the world, and who is the preserver of the throne of *khalifat*, written on the 27th of Ziqád in the 9th year of his Jalús, that mauzas *Mustipur*, *Táradih* are conferred upon Lal Gir Sannyási as *madad mash* without any restriction of names and divisions from the middle of *bijiail*, and as it is herewith prescribed. You all should, in obedience to the order, leave the said mauzas in his possession without making any change or alteration thereon, and should in no way be overcome by any kind of temptation, and should in all respect look upon the order as just and right, so that all the produce of the said property be used by him for his own livelihood and that of the itinerant faqirs; for which act of benevolence he should always pray for the stability of the wealth (of his Majesty). You all should not take notice of other properties belonging to the grantee. You all should take great care in carrying out the above orders.

Written on the 11th day of Rabiulawal in the 9th year of the August Jalús.

Appendix 2

List of immoveable property belonging to the Math of Bodh Gayá, District Gayá.

Serial Number.	Districts.	Pargana.	Tauzi number.
1	Gayá	Maher	..
2	Do.	Do.	...
3	Do.	Sherghâti ...	...
4	Do.	Ditto ...	...
5	Shahabad	Chainpur ...	...
6	Gayá	Sherghâti ...	...
7	Do.	Ditto ...	...
8	Do.	Ditto ...	...
9	Do.	Ditto ...	...
10	Do.	Ditto ...	...
11	Do.	Ditto ...	...
12	Do.	Ditto ...	...
13	Do.	Ditto ...	...
14	Do.	Ditto ...	...
15	Do.	Ditto ...	...
16	Do.	Ditto ...	...
17	Do.	Ditto ...	...
18	Do.	Ditto ...	...
19	Do.	Ditto ...	...
20	Do.	Ditto ...	...
21	Do.	Ditto ...	...
22	Do.	Ditto ...	...
23	Do.	Ditto ...	...
24	Do.	Ditto ...	..
25	Do.	Ditto ...	...
26	Do.	Ditto ...	...
27	Do.	Ditto ...	...
28	Do.	Ditto ...	...
29	Do.	Ditto ...	...
30	Do.	Ditto ...	...
31	Do.	Ditto ...	...
32	Do.	Ditto ...	...
33	Do.	Ditto ...	...
34	Do.	Ditto ...	...
35	Do.	Ditto ...	...
36	Do.	Ditto ...	...

Appendix 2

Name of property.	Sadar jams.	Road and public works cesses.	Dák cess.	Gross rental.	REMARKS.
	Rs. A. P.	Rs. A. P.	Rs. A. P.	Rs. A. P.	
The great Mahábodhi temple, together with tank, the peepul tree, and of the holy shrines and spots within its ambit, situated in mauza Mastipur Taradih.	...	...	...	...	No fixed in-come.
Mastipur and Taradih	...	...	...	900 4 6	Lákhiraj.
Mauza Ram Sagar Bagula	...	...	...	230 15 0	Ditto.
„ „ Dharahra Khurd ...	...	...	...	251 8 0	Ditto.
„ Ataria	...	...	...	315 0 0	Ditto.
„ Ram Sagar...	...	...	...	45 0 0	Ditto.
„ Hardaspur	...	...	...	75 0 0	Ditto.
„ Sagasot	...	...	...	148 0 0	Ditto.
„ Gojra	...	...	...	67 3 9	Ditto.
„ Harha Harhi	...	...	...	76 0 3	Ditto.
„ Mohammada alias Bhagwanpur	...	...	...	144 11 6	Ditto.
„ Bhanwar Bar	...	...	...	325 0 0	
„ Gogapur	...	...	...	355 15 9	
„ Shahbázar	...	...	...	88 4 3	
„ Pertappur	...	...	...	207 0 3	
„ Salaia	...	...	...	82 7 0	
„ Rajan	...	...	...	348 13 9	
„ Ram Sagar Pesra	...	...	...	265 7 0	
„ „ Tolaia	...	...	...	152 4 3	
„ Kharagpur (half)	...	...	...	122 8 0	
„ Ohak Thawai	...	...	...	43 0 0	
Arazi in mauza Sonhathy	...	...	...	43 4 3	
„ Pandea, mauza Pandea	...	...	...	16 10 9	
Chak Pandea Khairats	...	...	...	33 2 3	
Arazi Biraj Chak in mauza Rondwa ...	...	...	...	48 7 0	
„ Dumri Dumra Nowadih in mauza Chuabar.	...	...	...	27 15 3	
Arazi Pathak Chak in manza Sinduar ...	...	...	...	43 0 0	
„ Jainagar in mauza Ghogwa ...	...	...	...	75 0 0	
„ Budi in mauza Wari	...	...	...	15 1 6	
„ Darbar	...	...	...	226 10 9	
„ Pandea Khairat mauza Pandea	...	...	...	38 9 0	
„ Majhar in mauza Chunbar ...	...	...	...	9 13 6	
„ Balgara in mauza Rondwa ...	...	...	...	8 6 6	
„ Duhobar in mauza Duhobar ...	...	...	...	6 0 0	
„ Mauza Majhar in mauza Majhar	...	...	...	5 8 0	
„ Joribigha in mauza Khaira ...	...	...	...	15 0 0	

Serial Number.	Districts.	Pargana.	Tauzi number.
37	Do.	Ditto ...	...
38	Do.	Ditto ...	...
39	Do.	Ditto ...	...
40	Do.	Ditto ...	...
41	Do.	Ditto ...	...
42	Do.	Ditto ...	...
43	Do.	Ditto ...	...
44	Do.	Ditto ...	...
45	Do.	Sanaut	...
46	Do.	Pachrukhi	...
47	Do.	Maher	...
48	Do.	Do.	...
49	Do.	Do.	...
50	Do.	Do.	...
51	Do.	Do.	...
52	Do.	Do.	...
53	Do.	Do.	...
54	Do.	Do.	...
55	Do.	Do.	...
56	Do.	Do.	...
57	Do.	Do.	...
58	Do.	Do.	...
59	Do.	Do.	...
60	Gayá	Maher	...
61	Do.	Do.	...
62	Do.	Do.	...

Appendix 2

Name of property.	Sadar jams.	Road and public works cesses.	Dák cess.	Gross rental.	REMARKS.
	Rs. A. P.	Rs. A. P.	Rs. A. P.	Rs. A. P.	
„ Musargabda...	...	...	...	21 0 0	
„ Salempur	...	...	...	17 0 0	
Chak Sawai in mauza Amaroot	...	...	...	63 0 0	
Arazi Gangi in mauza Ghogwa	...	...	...	51 12 3	
„ Natha in mauza Naha	...	...	...	38 12 3	
„ Kenari in taluka Pankerdih Malabri	...	...	...	35 0 0	
Arazi Bamdhan Bigha in mauza Dharampur.	...	...	...	36 0 0	
„ Dewri in mauza Khaira	...	...	...	30 7 0	
„ Deodbarpur with the tank at Teknri and Arazi Lao.	...	...	...	71 0 0	
„ Gazipur	...	...	...	75 10 0	
Mauza Babhni	...	...	...	235 3 0	
„ Sukhwara	...	...	...	451 14 3	
Arazi Birabandh in mauza Mankosi ...	...	...	...	75 0 0	
„ Dandharpur Ghoghwa	...	...	...	131 0 0	
„ Kurumdih in mauza Anita ...	...	...	...	16 0 0	
„ Bari Bagh with Math Maltangi and in mauza, &c., Barkror.	...	...	...	100 0 0	
„ Girdhari bagh in mauza Barkror	...	...	...	19 0 0	
„ Proria ghat in mauza Bndhua	...	...	...	50 0 0	
„ Amawan in mauza Amawan ...	...	...	...	51 0 0	
„ Mahabodh in mauza Mahabodh	...	...	...	134 11 0	
„ Dhondhwa in mauza Dhondhwa	...	...	...	41 0 0	
„ Bagodar in mauza Dharampur ...	...	...	...	16 0 0	
„ Madhuram Bigha in mauza Mora.	...	...	...	25 0 0	
Arazi Dahria bigha with Muth, &c., in mauza Mabahodh.	...	...	...	5 0 0	
Araziin several plot in mauza Mocha-rim Katorwa. Ratnapura in mahal Ladu. B. K. D. DH. 1st plot Measuring ... 75 14 0 0 2nd „ „ ... 35 0 0 0 3rd „ „ ... 87 10 0 0 4th „ „ ... 65 0 0 0 5th „ „ ... 62 7 0 0 6th „ „ ... 60 3 0 0 7th „ „ ... 58 16 2 0 8th „ „ ... 66 0 0 0 9th „ „ ... 15 0 0 0 525 10 2 0	...	...	...	664 0 0	
Soorajpur Bardiha	...	...	...	16 8 0	

Serial Number.	Districts.	Pargana.	Tauzi number.
63	Do.	Pahra	434
64	Do.	Sherghâti	4706
65	Do.	Ditto ...	4404
66	Do.	Ditto ...	4624
67	Do.	Ditto ..	4616
68	Do.	Ditto	4764
69	Do.	Ditto ...	4568
70	Do.	Ditto ...	4614
71	Do.	Ditto ...	4674
72	Do.	Ditto ...	4672
73	Do.	Ditto ...	4521
74	Do.	Ditto ...	4452
75	Do.	Ditto ...	4674
76	Do.	Ditto ...	4674
77	Do.	Ditto ...	4780
78	Do.	Ditto ...	4581
79	Do.	Ditto ...	4711
80	Do.	Ditto ...	4508
81	Do.	Ditto ...	4674
82	Do.	Ditto ...	4674
83	Do.	Ditto ...	4674
84	Do.	Ditto ...	4674
85	Do.	Ditto ...	4674
86	Do.	Ditto ...	4520
87	Do.	Ditto ...	4674
88	Do.	Ditto ...	4674
89	Do.	Ditto ...	4587
90	Do.	Ditto ...	4687
91	Do.	Ditto ...	4727
92	Do.	Ditto ...	4568
93	Do.	Ditto ...	4432
94	Do.	Ditto ...	3228
95	Do.	Ditto ...	3289
96	Do.	Ditto ...	3189
97	Do.	Ditto ...	...
98	Do.	Ditto ...	...
99	Do.	Ditto ...	...
100	Do.	Ditto ...	...
101	Do.	Ditto ...	...
102	Do.	Ditto ...	...
103	Do.	Ditto ...	...
104	Do.	Ditto ...	...
105	Do.	Ditto ...	...
106	Do.	Ditto ...	...

Appendix 2

Name of property.	Sadar jams.	Road and public works cesses.	Dák cess.	Gross rental.	REMARKS.
	Rs. A. P.	Rs. A. P.	Rs. A. P.	Rs. A. P.	
Dhanawan	...	...	...	621 2 0	
Rondwa 4 mannas	44 0 0	...	...	125 0 0	Nizamat.
Mauza Sinduar, 10 annas 8 ples	187 12 0	...	...	600 0 0	Ditto.
„ Mauza Math Bumair	150 8 0	...	...	301 0 0	Ditto.
„ Ledhi	60 10 0	...	...	168 0 0	Ditto.
„ Udai Khop	26 4 0	...	...	63 0 0	Ditto
„ Jhalar	156 12 0	...	...	300 0 0	Ditto.
„ Lai Nagahra	236 13 0	...	...	781 0 0	Ditto.
Mansa Bigha Palebar	609 9 0	...	...	292 3 3	Ditto.
Pathra alias Pathal Garh	78 0 0	...	...	250 4 9	Ditto.
Mauza Dadoobarma	211 4 0	..	...	1,153 6 0	Ditto.
„ Bela Murdiha	380 12 0	...	...	663 15 0	Ditto.
„ Hasanpur in mauza Pindra ...	...	...	...	232 15 6	Ditto.
„ Ohatura Khap	609 9 0	...	...	131 0 0	Ditto.
„ Samda, 10 annas share	95 9 0	...	...	407 0 0	Ditto.
„ Kurmawan	236 13 0	...	...	440 8 3	Ditto.
„ Sahno	21 5 0	...	...	38 15 6	Ditto.
„ Chauria Bigha	74 14 0	...	...	173 4 6	Ditto.
„ Kusa	609 9 0	...	...	178 6 0	Ditto.
„ Bija	609 9 0	...	...	152 10 9	Ditto.
„ Kubalat Pindra	609 9 0	...	...	300 0 0	Ditto.
„ Suraundha	609 9 0	...	...	244 13 0	Ditto.
„ Kalaua	609 9 0	...	...	36 0 0	Ditto.
„ Dakhiu Khap	95 0 0	...	...	246 14 0	Ditto.
„ Palehat	609 9 0	...	...	109 2 3	Ditto.
„ Pindra and others	609 9 0	...	...	501 0 0	Ditto.
„ Kururudih, 5 annas 4 pies ...	11 15 0	...	...	55 0 0	Ditto.
„ Jhajh	12 15 0	...	...	36 7 6	Ditto.
„ Suggi	18 3 0	...	...	38 0 0	Ditto.
„ Bundabigha, half in mauza Jalor.	5 15 0	...	...	38 0 0	Ditto.
„ Gambira Lat Binda, 4 annas ...	12 8 0	...	...	85 0 0	Ditto.
„ Turi Kalan	135 9 0	...	...	380 9 3	Ditto.
„ Turi Khurd	130 0 0	...	...	339 11 7	Ditto.
„ Manikpur	15 0 0	...	...	200 0 0	Ditto.
„ Manik Diha	...	...	...	301 0 0	Ditto.
„ Katra	...	...	...	1,014 0 0	Ditto.
„ Gopal Kera	...	...	...	31 1 6	Ditto.
„ Goat alias Daha	...	...	...	19 11 3	Ditto.
„ Piprahi	...	...	...	89 2 6	Ditto.
„ Lalpur	...	...	...	90 2 0	Ditto.
„ Madar	...	...	...	229 6 0	Ditto.
„ Jamuni	...	...	...	65 0 0	Ditto.
„ Paharpur	...	...	...	2,222 8 6	Ditto.
„ Dumrichatti Gohra	...	...	...	1,516 5 9	Ditto.

Serial Number.	Districts.	Pargana.	Tauzi number.
107	Do.	Ditto	...
108	Do.	Ditto ...	...
109	Do.	Ditto ...	...
110	Do.	Ditto ...	...
111	Do.	Ditto ...	...
112	Do.	Ditto ...	...
113	Do.	Ditto ...	...
114	Do.	Maher ...	...
115	Do.	Do. ...	...
116	Do.	Do. ...	...
117	Do.	Do. ...	...
118	Do.	Do. ...	...
119	Do.	Do. ...	...
120	Do.	Do. ...	...
121	Patna	Haveli Bihar	247
122	Do.	Ditto ...	634
123	Gaya	Maher ...	...
124	Do.	Do. ...	...
125	Do.	Do. ...	...
126	Do.	Do. ...	...
127	Do.	Do. ...	...
128	Do.	Pahra ...	...
129	Do.	Maher ...	...
130	Do.	Do. ...	...
131	Do.	Do. ...	...
132	Do.	Do. ..	...
133	Do.	Do.	..
134	Do.	Do.	...
135	Do.	Do.	...
136	Do.	Do.	...
137	Do.	Do.	...
138	Do.	Do.	...
139	Do.	Do.	...
140	Do.	Do.	...
141	Do.	Do.	...
142	Do.	Do.	...
143	Do.	Do.	...
144	Do.	Do.	...
145	Do.	Do.	...
146	Do.	Do.	...
147	Do.	Do.	...
148	Do.	Do.	...
149	Do.	Do.	...
150	Do.	Do.	...

Appendix 2

Name of property.	Sadar jams.	Road and public works cesses.	Dák cess.	Gross rental.	REMARKS.
	Rs. A. P.	Rs. A. P.	Rs. A. P.	Rs. A. P.	
,, Bharay	...	...	...	720 2 3	Ditto.
,, Ghanto	...	...	...	65 0 0	Ditto.
,, Baraila Lat Dumri Kalan	..	...	...	551 0 0	Ditto.
,, Bagahi Khurd	...	..	...	217 0 0	Ditto.
,, Rajaundha	...	...	...	25 0 0	Ditto.
,, Raja Bigha, 4 annas share ...	...	...	...	25 4 0	Ditto.
,, Parsawan	...	...	...	180 4 3	Ditto.
,, Neotapur	...	...	...	64 5 3	Ditto.
,, Jagarnathpur	...	...	...	565 0 0	Ditto.
,, Chakmian bigha in mauza Jagarnathpur.	...	...	...	45 0 0	Ditto.
,, Poa Khas	...	...	...	1,055 0 0	Ditto.
,, Zindapur	...	...	...	186 12 3	Ditto.
,, Uz Rakha Diawan	...	...	...	75 0 0	
,, Dumri Kalan alias Raghopur ...	...	...	...	319 7 9	
,, Jiar	1,834 3 0	...	...	4,200 0 0	
,, Salempur Deokali	137 12 0	...	...	500 0 0	Mukarari.
,, Pandaria in Mahal Ladu ...	...	...	...	1,737 0 0	Ditto.
Arazi Pandaria in Mahal Ladu	...	...	...	49 0 0	Ditto.
,, Kulhaura	...	...	...	36 0 0	Ditto.
,, Anita Pandaria	...	...	...	125 0 0	Ditto.
,, Dhondhwa	...	...	...	61 0 0	Ditto.
Mauza Kendua Khiriawan	...	...	...	7,269 7 0	Ditto.
Arazi Paranpur in mahal Amawan ...	...	...	...	81 0 0	Ditto.
,, Jagarnathpur in Amawan ...	...	...	...	49 0 0	Ditto.
,, Pidasin	...	...	...	1,369 13 0	Ditto.
,, Mocharim known as Sripur ...	...	...	...	257 14 3	Ditto.
,, Bhamdina	...	...	...	35 0 0	Ditto.
,, Teora in mahal Ladu khas ...	...	...	...	185 0 0	Ditto.
Mauza Ladu khas	...	...	...	2,616 12 0	Ditto.
,, Gaora, half...	...	...	...	151 0 0	Ditto.
,, Antia, 7 annas share	...	...	...	642 0 0	Ditto.
Arazi Chao...	...	...	...	79 15 9	Ditto.
,, Makhdumpur	...	...	...	245 0 0	Ditto.
Mauza Raja, Bigha Dhuba	...	...	...	429 6 6	Ditto.
,, Sohjana	...	...	...	298 7 6	Ditto
Arazi Dumri in mauza Budhaul Gortorwa in Ladu.	...	...	...	101 0 0	Ditto.
Mauza Budhaul Gortorwa in mauza Ladu.	...	...	...	610 0 0	Ditto.
Arazi Jarhari	...	...	...	161 0 0	Ditto.
,, Guriawan	...	...	...	41 0 0	Ditto.
,, Mocharim	...	...	...	41 3 0	Ditto.
Mauza Rajbar Parsowni	...	...	...	1,270 0 0	Ditto.
Arazi Bagwanpur...	...	...	...	105 8 0	Ditto.
,, Rampur	...	...	...	230 14 9	Ditto.
Mauza Diawan	...	...	...	1,656 10 6	Ditto.

Serial Number.	Districts.	Pargana.	Tauzi number.
151	Do.	Do. ...	...
152	Gayá	Maher	...
153	Do.	Do.	...
154	Do.	Do.	...
155	Hazáribágh ...	Dantar and Chai ...	...
156	Ditto ...	Ditto ..	...
157	Ditto ...	Ditto ...	...
158	Ditto ...	Ditto ...	...
159	Ditto ...	Ditto ...	...
160	Ditto ...	Ditto ...	...
161	Ditto ...	Ditto ...	...
162	Ditto ...	Ditto ...	...
163	......	......	...
164	......	......	...
165	......	......	...
166	......	......	...
167	......	......	...
168	......	......	...
169	......	......	...
170	......	......	...
171	......	Ahuri	...
172	......	......	...
173	......	Chai	...
174	......	......	...
175	Surguja	Suraguja and Jaspur	...
176	......	......	...
177	......	......	...
178	......	......	...
179	......	......	...
180	......	......	...
181	......	......	...
182	......	......	...
183	......	......	...
184	......	......	...
185	......	......	...
186	......	......	...
187	Surguja	Suraguja and Jaspur	...
188	......	......	...
189	......	......	...
190	......	......	...
191	......	......	...
192	......	......	...
193	......	.....	...

Appendix 2

Name of property.	Sadar jams.	Road and public works cesses.	Dák cess.	Gross rental.	REMARKS.
	Rs. A. P.	Rs. A. P.	Rs. A. P.	Rs. A. P.	
,, Khaira	...	...	...	59 3 6	Ditto.
Arazi Pipra in mauza Makhdumpur ...	...	...	...	125 0 0	Mukarari.
Mauza Tutuia	...	...	...	275 0 0	Ditto.
Arazi Mora Ratnara, alias Gaugabigha	...	...	...	13 8 0	Ditto.
Mauza Kirani	...	...	...	51 10 0	Lukhiraj.
,, Dhebo	...	...	...	175 0 0	Ditto.
,, Tetaria	...	...	...	38 0 0	Ditto.
,, Snerpur	...	...	...	52 0 0	Ditto.
,, Sonbarsa	...	...	...	175 0 0	Ditto.
,, Amın	...	...	...	217 1 0	Ditto.
,, Bhagwanpur	...	...	...	96 12 0	Ditto.
,, Simaria	...	...	...	110 6 9	Ditto.
,, Gosaindih	...	...	...	401 0 0	
,, Banka	...	...	...	241 0 0	
,, Balgara	...	...	...	74 6 0	
,, Nareha Khairat half, and mauza Nareha Kalan.	...	...	...	412 6 9	
,, Dariapur mauza Guri, Khariat Nareha half.	...	...	...	407 7 9	
Mauza Lalklshun chak, Ichak	...	...	...	150 10 0	
,, Banıan tand, Selodhar	...	...	...	151 0 0	
,, Banian bandh	...	...	...	45 0 0	
,, Pachmabla	...	...	...	67 0 6	
Arazi Chatra	...	...	...	41 0 0	
,, Mathwa taur in mauza chatra	...	...	...	7 7 0	
Mauza Sailpur	...	...	...	275 0 0	
Khajuri	...	...	...	407 0 0	
Udur Suhi	...	...	...	167 0 0	
Jamathi	...	...	...	46 0 0	
Mauza Umko	...	...	...	235 0 0	
,, Bakaspur	...	...	...	41 0 0	
,, Chainpur	...	...	...	61 0 0	
,, Nunera	...	...	...	61 0 0	
,, Sirikotanga	...	...	...	61 0 0	
,, Soni	...	...	...	30 0 0	
,, Dipa Dih	...	...	...	176 0 0	
,, Largi	...	...	...	48 0 0	
,, Jabra	...	...	...	160 0 0	
,, Silsila	...	...	...	126 0 0	
,, Amtahı	...	...	...	82 0 0	
,, Buta	...	...	...	11 0 0	
,, Ohhıchhiı	...	...	...	125 0 0	
,, Bodı	...	...	...	105 0 0	
,, Dhasma	...	...	...	125 0 0	
,, Bajur Suta	...	...	...	[illegible]	

Serial Number.	Districts.	Pargana.	Tauzi number.	
194	......	......	...	
195	......	......	...	
196	Surguja	Suraguja and Jaspur	...	
197	Ditto	Ditto ...	...	
198	Ditto	Ditto ...	...	
199	Ditto	Ditto ..	...	
200	Ditto	Ditto ..	...	
201	Shahabad... ...	Chainpur	...	
202	Hazáribágh ...	Todi	...	
203	Patna	Patna	...	
204	Gayá	Sherghátí	4403	
205	......	Maher	...	
206	......	......	...	
207	......	Pahrá	...	
208	......	......	...	
209	......	Sherghátí	...	
210	......	......	...	
211	......	Pahrá	...	
212	......	Maher	...	

Appendix 2

	Name of property.	Sadar jams.	Road and public works cesses.	Dák cess.	Gross rental.	REMARKS.
		Rs. A. P.	Rs. A. P.	Rs. A. P.	Rs. A. P.	
	,, Sondiha	...	...	...	33 0 0	
	,, Selauta	...	...	...	170 0 0	
	,, Bodi Kalan..	...	...	...	10 0 0	Lakhiraj.
	,, Sunwahi	...	...	...	32 0 0	Ditto.
	,, Galora	...	...	...	401 0 0	Ditto.
	,, Korja	...	...	...	101 0 0	Ditto.
	,, Sarima	...	...	...	101 0 0	Ditto.
	,, Jeori	...	...	...	601 0 0	Ditto.
	,, Dąmodar	...	...	...	175 0 0	Ditto.
	Arazi Lohanipur with arazi Moghalpara	20 3 0	...	...	37 0 0	Ditto.
	Mauza Akhay khap	...	...	...	38 15 6	Niznmat.
	,, Shiva Rajpur, 8 annas	...	...	...	250 0 0	
	Arazi 21 bighus in mauza Mocharim ...	...	...	...	125 0 0	Lakhiraj.
	,, Bhojo Bigha...	...	...	...	75 0 0	Jagir.
	,, Elara Dulara	...	...	...	65 0 0	
	Mauza chak Goharia	...	...	...	115 0 0	
	,, Bhat Bigha	...	...	...	125 0 0	
	Uz Rakba, Jatia jamdi, known as Gulni	...	...	...	290 0 0	
	Bodh Gaya dak bunglow	...	...	...	8 0 0	
		Total		...	59,004 9 10	

Appendix 3

Mobile View Calcutta High Court
Indian Kanoon—http://indiankanoon.org/doc/1821486/
Calcutta High Court
Jaipal Gir And Ors. vs H. Dharmapala on 22 August, 1895
Equivalent citations: (1896) ILR 23 Cal 60
Author: Macpherson
Bench: Macpherson, Banerjee
JUDGMENT

Macpherson, J.

1. The three petitioners, who are described as Hindu sannyasis of the monastery of Bodh-Gaya, have been convicted under Section 296 of the Penal Code of disturbing the worship of the complainant and other Buddhists of Ceylon in the temple of Mahabodhi at Bodh-Gaya on the 25th February last, and the conviction has been upheld by the Sessions Judge. They were tried and acquitted on other charges under Sections 295, 297 and 143.

2. The Magistrate says: "The case is one of importance, as the disturbance in sought to be justified by the defendants on the ground that their superior, the Mahant of Bodh-Gaya, claims the right, though a Hindu, of regulating what worship shall be performed in this famous shrine, known as the Great Temple of Mahabodhi, and regarded by the Buddhists, that is, by about one-third of the human race, as the most sacred spot on earth." That I think is rather misleading. No such broad question arises, and it is desirable to keep the case within its proper limits. It is for the complainant to prove that he and his co-religionists, when disturbed, were lawfully engaged in the performance of religious worship or religious ceremonies, a fact which the petitioners denied. The defence may have put their case higher than was necessary, but it is not right to say that it is the defence which gives the case its importance.

3. There is no doubt, however, that the case has attracted a good deal of attention from the prominence which has been given to it and from the nature of the dispute and the position of the parties. It has been fought with a persistency and at a cost which would have been more appropriate if it had been brought in a Court which could finally determine the rights of the parties, and not in a Criminal Court where the narrow issue is,

whether a criminal offence has been committed.

4. The trial has occupied a long time, leading Counsel have been retained, and very lengthy judgments, traversing the whole history of the temple, have been recorded. It may well be doubted whether the object of the complainant was not to do something much more than to punish a crime. It has been contended throughout that no criminal offence was committed, and, in the Appellate Court, that on the facts found there was no criminal offence. As it seemed to us very questionable if the conviction was right, we gave a rule to show cause why it should not be set aside, and the case has now been fully argued by the learned Counsel who argued it before the Sessions Judge. It was suggested, when the rule was applied for, that the petitioners had not a perfectly fair trial, as the learned Magistrate had formed an opinion, before this dispute took place, of the rights of the parties, which necessarily, but perhaps unconsciously, influenced his decision. We did not give a rule on that ground, and I think it right to say that, both in the conduct of the trial and in his very long and careful judgment, the Magistrate seams to have been scrupulously fair.

5. The facts connected with the occurrence of the 25th February are thus stated by the District Magistrate and not disputed. He says:

> Between 8 and 9 o'clock on the morning of that day the complainant, who is a Buddhist gentleman from Ceylon and Honorary General Secretary of the Mahabodhi Society, arrived at Bodh-Gaya with two Singhalese Buddhist priests, Sumangala and Devananda, and a layman, Silva, of the same race and religion, and proceeded to enshrine a highly artistic, and, it is said, historical image of Buddha, sent from Japan for the purpose, on the altar in the chamber of the upper floor of the Mahabodhi temple. While they were setting up the image two Mahomedan gentlemen, namely, the Special Sub-Registrar and Deputy Magistrate of Gaya, happened to come to see the place, and wore accompanied by a Mahomedan mukhtear of the Mahant of Bodh-Gaya named Hussain Baksh, and by one Jagannatb Singh, a Hindu door-keeper, whom the Mahant keeps at the temple. After they entered the chamber, Hussain Baksh said something to the latter, who thereupon left. The three Mahomedans also went away before all the paraphernalia of the image were set up. The image with censer, candlesticks and lotus flowers and also a Japanese dedicatory certificate, describing its history, was duly set up, and Dharmapala then sent word to the Government custodian of the temple, and, on his coming six or seven minutes after, put the image in his charge,

saying it had been sent by the Japanese. This done, Sumangala Look one of the candles to light it, but at that moment about thirty or forty of the Mahant's sannyasis and other Hindus, and also the mukhtear, Hussain Baksh, came rushing into the place in a very rowdy fashion. Some got on to the altar, a couple of them placed themselves between Dharmapala and it, one snatched the candle out of Sumangala's hand to prevent its being lit, and most spoke in a vehement and imperative tone, commanding Dharmapala to take away the image, and using such throats as budinash, we will beat you, there are five hundred of us. The Mahomedan in particular kept pushing him on the shoulder vehemently telling him to remove the image. The Government custodian, finding them much enraged, kept imploring them with folded hands not to act hastily. Dharmapala refused to remove the imago, and as he knows little of the language, a number of them went and fetched the Mahant's Hindu mukhtear, Vijayananda, who happened to be at the monastery in connection with a document of the Mahant's the Sub-Registrar had come to got registered. Dharmapala pointed out to Vijayananda what desecration it was for people to ho on the altar, and the latter got one or two to come down. Thereupon this mukhtear and all but a few, who remained quietly looking on, left the temple, and Dharmapala and the two priests, thinking all opposition had ended, sat down to their devotion in front of the image in the characteristic Buddhist attitude of religious contemplation, the highest form of Buddhist worship. They were absorbed in this form of devotion for about a quarter of an hour, when the Hindus again came to the temple, and heedless of their attitude, made a rush into the place and tumultuously carried off the image of Buddha and set it down in the open courtyard below. This tumult, and indeed the more removal of the imago itself, put an end to the devotional contemplation of the Buddhists. Dharmapala and one of the priests continued, however, to sit there, and in a few minutes a constable came up to call him down to the head constable, who had been sent for by the Government custodian, and to whom also the mukhtear, Hussain Baksh, had made a statement praying him to interfere. Dharmapala refused to go down, so the head constable had to come up whore he was, and began questioning him in Hindi; but Dharmapala, not understanding this, wrote down there and then, at his request, a summary statement of the occurrence.

6. I may add to them that the image and all its paraphernalia were conveyed in boxes to the chamber of the upper floor and opened there, that the doorkeeper, who was apparently the only person encountered, made

no opposition to the entry, and that neither the Mahant nor any one else connected with the temple, nor any Government Official, had been informed of the complainant Dhanuapala's intention to place the image there.

7. It may be conceded that the Mahabodhi temple, which is very ancient and very sacred to Buddhists, was a Buddhist, temple; that, although it has been in the possession of Hindu Mahants, it has never been converted into a Hindu temple in the sense that the Hindu idols have been enshrined or orthodox Hindu worship carried on there, and that Buddhist pilgrims have had free access and full liberty to worship in it. It does not appear that any hindrance was ever offered to them or that any complaints were ever made by them, and, before the occurrence in question, there is no instance of any disturbance between the Buddhist worshippers and the Hindu Mahants or their subordinates, in regard to their respective rights. This fact is of some importance in the present case, where each party charges the other with being the aggressor. The petitioners, no doubt, now say that the Buddhists worshipped by permission, and not of right. That is a question which it is unnecessary to consider. I shall assume for the purpose of this case that the worship which they were in the habit of performing was of right. It will, however, be necessary to consider the nature of that worship, and the nature of the act which gave rise to the disturbance complained of, in order to see whether a criminal offence has been committed.

8. A great part of the lengthy judgments of the Magistrate and of the Judge is devoted to a discussion of the Mahant's position in regard to the temple and the extent of his proprietary right and power of control. His possession is found, but the extent of his proprietary interest and power of control is questioned. It is quite unnecessary to discuss his proprietary interest. There is no doubt that he is in possession, that he is the sole superintendent of the temple, and that he takes all the offerings, both of Hindus and Buddhists; and the present state of things appears to have been in existence for many years, if not for centuries. It is not proved, I do not think it is even alleged, that any Buddhist priests have ever exercised any control or authority in the temple within living memory. The Government has had no occasion to interfere in the internal management, even if it could do so, and that is not a question which need be considered in this case. If the control and superintendence of the temple is not vested in the Mahant, it does not appear to be vested in any one

9. The Judge seems to think that the Mahant placed some limitation on

his own rights or powers by the agreement entered into in 1877 with the representative of the King of Burma. This agreement and the translation of it will be found at page 107 of the paper book, part I. The correctness of the translation of the third passage, referred to in the Judge's judgment, is a matter of dispute, but the Judge in his translation has omitted to give any effect to the word hamare in the passage uski puja hamate shudamad-i-qadeem se chali ati hai. It may or may not be that that agreement has some bearing on the question whether Buddhists worship by permission or of right, and which, as I have said, is now immaterial; but neither the agreement nor the subsequent appointment of a Government custodian, whose principal duty it apparently is to look after the building and relics generally, have, I consider, made any difference in the Mahant's position for the purposes of this case. That position 1 find to be this, that he held possession of the temple and had the control and superintendence over it, subject to that right of Buddhists to worship there in the customary manner, that is to say, in the manner in which they had been in the habit of worshipping. I see nothing in the judgments of the lower Courts which goes against this finding. The difficulty is to understand from those judgments where the freedom of worship ends and the right of control begins.

10. The question really is whether the freedom of worship enjoyed by the Buddhists covered what Dharmapala and his associates did. It is for the hitter to bring the case strictly within the four corners of Section 296, and prove that they were, when disturbed, lawfully engaged in the performance of religious worship or religious ceremonies.

11. The petitioners say that they were not so engaged, that what they did was something which had never been done before, and that it was done, not for the purpose of religious worship, but for another object, in the assertion of a right and with the knowledge that they would be resisted. This renders it necessary to consider in some detail the nature of the act done and resisted, and the nature of the worship which the Buddhists were in the habit of doing.

12. Dharmapala was subjected to a very long cross-examination on his denial that the Mahant was either the owner or the person in possession of the temple. Whatever excuses may be made for him, he certainly came very badly out of it, and furnished the other side with good grounds for questioning his general veracity. It is amply shown from his own writings, and from writings published with his knowledge and under his authority, that he always regarded the Mahant, whatever the latter's strict rights may be,

as the owner. Dharmapala was not in the position of an ordinary devotee, worshipping at the shrine. He was undoubtedly a religious enthusiast and an agitator. I use the word in no offensive sense, for I may freely concede that he was thoroughly sincere in his religious views and in promoting the work which he had undertaken. He was the Secretary of the Mahabodhi Society, which was started in Ceylon in May 1891, and also the editor of a monthly journal started to promote the objects of the Society. One of the objects of the Society was, he admits, to recover the possession of the Mahabodhi temple from the Mahant, and the prospectus moots the idea "of restoring the central shrine and transferring it from the hands of the usurping Saivite Mahants to the custody of the Buddhist monks." Numerous extracts from the journal, which were put in, show that the object was to establish Buddhist control in the temple. In February 1893, he and Colonel Olcott, an Honorary Director of the Society, interviewed the Mahant with the view of acquiring the religious custody of the temple for the Buddhists of all nations, but the Mahant, as the correspondence shows, refused either to sell or give a lease on any terms. Dharmapala then, according to a letter addressed to the President of the Society and signed by himself and Colonel Olcott, began to enquire into the legality of the Mahant's tenure. In 1893, when in Japan promoting the objects of the Society, he conceived the idea of enshrining a new image of Buddha in the temple, as there was, he says, no image in the upper floor chamber, which he regarded as the sanctum sanctorum. The result was that the image in question was sent to him in March 1894 It is described as a beautiful work of art, and it was accompanied by a dedicatory certificate addressed to him by the High Priest of Tokio. It is there described as a very ancient and holy image, and it was presented "to be enshrined in the second storey of the Bodh-Gaya Temple."

13. Dharmapala announced in his journal that the image would be placed in the temple on the 19th May, a very holy day with Buddhists, in the presence of the Collector. There was no authority for the latter part of the announcement, and the Mahant had not been consulted. The latter, learning of the intended installation by Dharmapala, objected to it and closed the temple door to prevent it. This he afterwards opened in compliance with an order of the District Magistrate made under Section 144 of the Criminal Procedure Code. It was mentioned in the order that no image would be set up in the temple that night without the Mahant's consent, and the Magistrate at the same time sent a demi-official letter to Dharmapala, in consequence of which he desisted from placing the image.

14. In April 1894 Dharmapala invoked the assistance of the Bengal Government in aid of the Mahabodhi Society, and received, in reply, the letter Exhibit D. 22, which he produced. This is dated the 5th May. In it he is informed that the Lieutenant-Governor can take no measures for the furtherance of the general objects of the Mahabodhi Society, that there is perfect freedom of worship for all Buddhists at Bodh-Gaya, and that any well-grounded complaint that difficulties were imposed would meet with ready attention and redress at the hands of the Bengal Government.

15. In June 1894 he again addressed the Lieutenant-Governor, complaining as he says, of the refusal to allow the image to be placed in the temple. He denies that he asked for help or Government influence. In reply, he received the letter, Exhibit D. 23, from the Chief Secretary, dated 22nd June. In it he is told that the Government must decline to exercise any influence with the Mahant of the Bodh-Gaya shrine, and he is referred to the letter Exhibit

16. In June 1894 he also petitioned the Magistrate on the subject of the Japanese image, and was informed in September (Exhibits D. 28a and D. 28b) that the local authorities could not deal with the matter.

17. Nothing more happened till the morning of the 25th February 1895, when he went surreptitiously, as the Judge says, to set up the. image in the upper chamber, and the occurrence took place of which he now complains. He says he did not anticipate opposition, but it is impossible to believe this. He had no reason to believe that the opposition bad ceased, and he bad every reason to believe that, as his position and motives became better known, the opposition to his doing anything which might lead to give him a better foothold in the temple would be more intense.

18. I have said that Dharmapala was not in the position of an ordinary devotee, but he is, of course, entitled to have the legality of his act judged as if he was -one. He could do as much, but no more, and if his act was in itself lawful, his previous failure and his failure to get the assistance of the Bengal Government (sic)of the local executive officers would not make it any the less so. But his petition and his past conduct are of importance in judging of his motives and the motives which led to the opposition.

19. Now what Dharmapala wanted and attempted to do was to enshrine this image in the upper room of the temple against the will of the Mahant, in whose possession and under whose superintendence the temple was, and there is no doubt that it was the attempted enshrinement which led to the

disturbance. The Judge, whose judgment I have felt some difficulty in following, takes exception to the word "enshrine" which the Magistrate uses, as he says there is no evidence that the Buddhists intended permanently to enshrine the image that day. It seems to me that no other conclusion is possible. The image had been obtained for enshrinement in the upper chamber, and it was sent for that purpose, as the dedicatory certificate, which was placed alongside it, shews. Moreover, Dharmapala, when putting it up, sent for the custodian, Bebin Behary, and said, "this present from the Japanese Government is now placed on the shrine, and now it is under your control." This clearly shews that he intended it to remain there. If he merely intended to do an act of worship before it, and then remove it, why did he go surreptitiously to the upper chamber? Giving him credit also for the religious feeling which he claims to have, it is absurd to suppose that he was indifferent to the fate of this image, if the Mahant afterwards removed, it, although the course which he might have taken in such an event is a matter of conjecture. It does not appear that there is any special ceremony connected with the enshrinement of an image; but, however that may be, I have no doubt that Dharmapala's object was to make the altar of the upper room the permanent shrine of this image.

20. As regards motive the Judge says that the Mahant had no ground for anticipating any injury to his interest from the act of Dharmapala, and that there was no ground for inferring any connection between the known and published desire of the Buddhists and the Mahabodhi Society, in connection with the temple, and the setting up this image as an object of temporary or permanent worship. His final conclusion is that Dharmapala's immediate object was "to gain a spiritual triumph for Buddhism, and to get rid of a responsibility, which, although he had sought it himself in the greatest hope and confidence, he now felt was an intolerable burden." The spiritual triumph meant doing what he originally intended to do, and in the face of opposition; and as for the burden, a man cannot be allowed to relieve himself by doing a wrong, and then complaining that he has been resisted. As regards the connection above referred to, I think there was reasonable ground for inferring a connection. The Mahant certainly seems to have thought so in 1894, probably much more in 1895. Dharmapala has no cause for surprise if his intentions and motives were misconstrued. Now I think Dharmapala has failed to shew that he had any right to do what he did against the known will of the Mahant, or that he went to perform a religious worship or a religious ceremony of a kind which was customary with Buddhist worshippers at the temple.

21. It is said, and no doubt, with truth, that to enshrine an image of Buddha, or to place such an image on an altar and sit before it in contemplation, are high forms of Buddhist worship, but the image must be placed where there is a right to place it. There was no image of Buddha in the upper chamber, and, whatever may have been the case in remote ages, none can speak to ever having seen such an image there, and there is no evidence that Buddhist worshippers generally used to go to that chamber for worship. At the time of this disturbance, and both before and after the restoration of the temple, there was a large image of Buddha in the shrine on the ground floor of the temple, and before this Buddhist devotees used to worship and make offerings. They seem to have been content with this, and before Dharmapala came, no one wanted to do anything more. He himself has worshipped many times before the great image since 1891, without any opposition, and he says he had no reason to be dissatisfied with it as everything about it was right. He also says that he has no knowledge of any Buddhist having attempted to enshrine an image in the upper chamber. There is evidence, upon which reliance is placed, that Burmese pilgrims in November and December 1891. placed some marble images of Buddha by the big image on the altar downstairs without asking the Mahant's permission. That may be so, and it is clear that the Mahant did not object, but what was then done was in no way analogous to what was done here. The Mahant, in whose possession the temple is, objected to Dharmapala's enshrining this image in the upper floor of the temple, and there is nothing on the evidence to justify the Court in holding that the right to place it there existed, or that the Mahant's objection could be disregarded. Dharmapala may possibly be able to establish the right which he asserts, but that is a question for another tribunal. It is enough to say that he has not proved it in this case so as to justify his act.

22. The evidence shows, and the Magistrate finds, that since July 1894, the Mahant and his disciples have been carrying on a sort of spurious Hindu worship of the great image of Buddha on the altar of the ground floor, and that the image has been dressed in a way which renders it repugnant to Buddhist worshippers. The Magistrate regards this as a stratagem on the Mahant's part to strengthen his position against, I suppose, some threatened danger. This was extremely wrong, but it does not, I think, affect the present case. In January 1895 Dharmapala and a party of pilgrims worshipped before the great image after removing the vestments and obliterating the tilah marks, and no objection was made to their doing this. The Mahant's conduct does not seem to have been made the subject of any remonstrance to him or of complaint to any one else, and it

cannot be said to have led to Dharmapala's action on the 25th February. That the Mahant really believed that his possession was threatened by Dharmapala, whose views with reference to the temple must have been well known, I cannot doubt, and it is impossible to say that there was not some ground for the belief. The desire to enshrine the Japanese image in the upper floor of the temple, where no image had been before, may have been very laudable from a purely religious point of view, but it is at least open to doubt whether his motive was purely religious and not to further his known desire to bring the temple under Buddhist control. Anyhow, as he has not proved his right to put it there against the will of the Mahant, he has not shown that, when putting it, he was lawfully engaged in the performance of religious worship or religious ceremonies. It is said, however, that there were two disturbances with an interval between them, and that, oven if there was no disturbance of a lawful religious worship or ceremony on the first occasion, when Dharmapala was told to remove the image and was prevented from lighting the candles, there certainly was on the second, when the image was removed, as the Buddhists were then sitting in contemplation before the image and actually and to the knowledge of the disturbers engaged in religious worship. It is argued that the worship having commenced, they were lawfully engaged in it, and that, even if the petitioners had the right to remove the image before worship commenced or after it ended, the removal, of it during worship was a disturbance and an offence under Section 296. Several cases have been put by way of analogy, and I may concede that, if the petitioners, in effecting an object which they were legally entitled to affect, disturbed an assembly lawfully engaged in the performance of religious worship by means which they knew must disturb it, they would be guilty of an offence under Section 296, even if they had no intention of disturbing it. But it is quite clear that the worship referred to in Section 296 must be a real worship, and not a cloak for doing something else, and that the assembly must be lawfully engaged in worship. It is quite true that if I see persons in a posture of worship, it is no excuse for disturbing them to say that 1 thought they were not worshipping, and that they were thinking of something which they ought not to have been thinking about, but obviously much must depend upon the circumstances under which they were worshipping. Here I think it is quite open to the petitioners to say that there was no real worship, but I do not wish to decide the case on that ground, or to hold that the Buddhists were not really contemplating, and that they merely fell into a posture of worship for appearances' sake. 1 prefer to hold, as I do, that they were not lawfully engaged in worship, that the disturbance must be regarded as continuous, and that if they were not lawfully engaged at first they were not lawfully engaged afterwards. They went to enshrine an image in a place where they had no right to enshrine it. The enshrinement may have involved the performance of religious worship or religious ceremony, but their immediate object was to enshrine it and not simply to perform an act of worship. They wore told, before the enshrinement was complete, or before worship commenced, to remove the image, they were prevented from lighting the candles, and all the persons who went to interfere did not leave the room. Dharmapala Hays that sitting in contemplation before an image of Buddha is the highest form of Buddhist worship, but that there are other forms, the offering of flowers and the burning of candles being the preliminaries. He says they were not allowed to light the candles, and that "the prevention of the lighting of the candles was a disturbance of a part and parcel of our religious worship." If so, it was a disturbance from the first, and a disturbance which continued, and the mere circumstance of their falling into a posture of worship in front of the image which they had been ordered to remove, but before it actually was removed, an act which nothing but the use of personal violence could have prevented, does not put them in any better position than they were at first.

23. To say that there was at first no disturbance of their religious worship or ceremony which amounted to an offence, but that there was such a disturbance afterwards, is to put the case on very narrow grounds, and the answer is, I think, clear. For these reasons I hold that no offence has been committed under Section 296, which was never intended to apply to a case like this, and that the conviction must be set aside and the fine refunded.

24. It is greatly to be regretted that this criminal case should have been brought and pressed in the way it has been. Dharmapala's motive in bringing it is, I think, very questionable, and a perusal of his evidence, which is open to severe criticism, shows that he is responsible for the great length to which the trial has been prolonged.

Banerjee, J.

25. I am of the same opinion.

26. The accused in this case were convicted by the District Magistrate of Gaya of the offence of voluntarily causing disturbance to the complainant and his associates, who were found to have been lawfully engaged in the performance of religious ceremonies and religious worship in the Mahabodhi temple at Bodh-Gaya, and were sentenced under Section 296

of the Indian Penal Code to one month's simple imprisonment and a fine of Rs. 100 each.

27. On appeal by them the learned Sessions Judge has affirmed the convictions and the sentences of fine, but set aside the sentences of imprisonment.

28. They now ask us, in the exercise of our revisional powers, to set aside the convictions and sentences, on the ground that upon the facts as found by the Courts below and upon the facts disclosed by the evidence, no offence under Section 296 of the Indian Penal Code has been committed by them.

29. We have heard learned Counsel on both sides at some length and considered the evidence and the elaborate judgments of the Courts below, and the conclusion we have arrived at is that the contention of the petitioners is correct.

30. To constitute an offence under Section 296 of the Indian Penal Code-

(1) There must be a voluntary disturbance caused;

(2) The disturbance must be caused to an assembly engaged in religious worship or religious ceremonies; and

(3) The assembly must be lawfully engaged in such worship or ceremonies.

31. These being the ingredients necessary to constitute the offence, let us see how far the evidence establishes their existence.

32. The evidence which has been fully discussed in the judgment of my learned colleague, and which I need not therefore refer to at any length, taken along with certain books of public history, such as Martin's edition of Buchanan Hamilton's "Eastern India" and Rajendra Lala Mitra's "Buddha-Gaya," which may be referred to under Section 57 of the Evidence Act, proves the following facts:

(1) The great temple at Bodba-Gaya, said to occupy the site of Buddha's hermitage, was originally a Buddhist temple; but it has for a long time (how long it is neither easy nor necessary in this case exactly to determine, but certainly for more than a century) been in the possession and under the control of the Hindu Mahant of that place.

(2) Buddhist pilgrims have, however, from time to time, continued to visit the temple and perform their worship there; but there is no

reliable evidence to show that the upper chamber had in recent times been ever resorted to by Buddhisms. The temple has, however, not been shown to have been converted into a place of Hindu worship, though there is a spot in the temple compound, which is resorted to by Hindus as a sacred place for offering pindas or oblations to ancestors.

(3) Early in 1893 an endeavour was made on behalf of the Mahabodhi Society of Ceylon (established in 1891), of which the complainant Dbarmapala is the General Secretary, to obtain a conveyance or lease of the temple from the Mahant; and on the negotiations for the purchase or lease failing, the complainant, it seems, applied to the Government of Bengal in April 1894, requesting it to help the Mahabodhi Society in obtaining the transfer of the Bodha-Gaya temple from the Mahant, but was told in reply that the Government was not in a position to help him.

(4) In the meantime, in November 1893, the complainant obtained from Japan an image of Buddha, highly artistic in execution and said to be of historic importance, with a document purporting to be signed by the High Priest of Tokio, for the purpose of enshrinement in the second storey of the Bodha-Gaya temple, and "as a good sign" (as the document puts it) "for the success of the restoration of the Bodha-Gaya temple;" and he advertised in the Mahabodhi Society's journal that on the 19th of May 1894, in the presence of the Collector of Gaya, he would place that image in the temple; but he had to desist from placing the image there upon the objection of the Mahant and upon receipt of a prohibitory order from the Magistrate.

(5) No further attempt was made to place the Japanese image in the temple until the 25th of February 1895 (the day of the occurrence, which has given rise to this case), when between 8 and 9 in the morning the complainant with two other Singhalese priests and one Singhalese layman went with the image to the upper floor of the temple, and after they had set up the image on the altar and were about to light one of the candles, as a preliminary to their worship, a number of retainers of the Mahant came, snatched the candle away, and commanded the complainant to remove the image. After some expostulation all but a few left the temple; and Dharmapala and the two priests sat down to their devotion in front of the image in the characteristic Buddhist attitude of religious contemplation, when in about a quarter of an hour a number of men, including the accused,

came and tumultuously carried off the image and set it down in the open courtyard below.

33. As regards the first of these facts, the complainant professes not to be aware of the Mahant's right to, or possession of, the temple; but he is contradicted by his own writings in the journal of the Mahabodhi Society, and by his own conduct in seeking to obtain a conveyance or a lease of the temple from the Mahant. The shuffling nature of his evidence has been unfavourably commented upon in the judgments of both the Courts below, and the learned Sessions Judge, in order to reconcile his view of the general truthfulness of Dharmapala's evidence with the unreliable character of this part of it, has to rely upon the erroneous and somewhat mischievous theory of the oriental standard of truth being different from the normal standard, a theory, the application of which must often lead, as it has in this instance led, to incorrect estimation of evidence. I deem it right here to observe that the question what the exact nature and extent of the Mahant's control over the temple is, the evidence adduced in the case does not enable us to determine.

34. With reference to the second fact, it was urged on behalf of the petitioners that the Buddhists cannot claim it as a matter of right to worship in the temple, and that they have hitherto done so only by the permission of the Mahant; but I do not think it necessary to determine the point in this case.

35. Touching the remaining three facts, there was practically not much dispute.

36. These being the facts of the case, Mr. Ghose, for the petitioners, contended that they disprove the existence of the three ingredients necessary to constitute the offence of which the petitioners have been convicted.

37. He contended first of all that it was evident from facts 1, 3 and 4, and from the finding of the District Magistrate, which was fully borne out by the evidence and had been erroneously set aside by the Judge, that the accused, in removing the image which had been placed in the temple by the complainant in the assertion of a right he did not possess and in denial of the Mahant's rights, acted under a bonâ fide belief that they were only defending the rights of the Mahant without any intention of disturbing any one; and that they cannot therefore be said to have voluntarily caused any disturbance. Having regard to the definition of the word "voluntarily" as given in Section 39 of the Indian Penal Code, I do

not think this contention is correct. Intention to cause a certain result is not an element necessary to constitute a voluntary causing of that result, but knowledge of, or belief in, the likelihood of the result following, though not intended, may supply the place of intention. If, therefore, the accused knew, or had reason to believe that their act in removing the image was likely to cause disturbance to any religious worship, then, though they might not have intended to cause such disturbance, yet the causing of the disturbance would be voluntary within the meaning of the Penal Code. There would no doubt still remain the question whether the accused knew or had reason to believe that the complainant and his companions were engaged in religious worship at the time, and that their act in removing the image was likely to cause disturbance of such worship. But, having regard to the position of the accused as members of a religious fraternity and to the means they enjoyed of observing Buddhist worship in the temple, which lies close to their monastery, I am not prepared to dissent from the conclusion arrived at by the Courts below that this question should be answered in the affirmative.

38. The learned Counsel for the petitioners next contended that the religious worship and religious ceremonies which Section 296 of the Indian Penal Code contemplates, must be real religious worship and real religious ceremonies, and not such as are colourable only, and that the worship and ceremonies which the complainant and his party were engaged in, were merely a pretext to cover their act of asserting their right against the claims of the Mahant. Whilst admitting fully the correctness of the first branch of this contention, that the religious worship and ceremonies contemplated by the section must be such as are real, and conceding also that the previous acts and conduct of the complainant, as proved by his own writings in the journal of the Maha-bodhi Society, tend to show that his action on the 25th of February 1895 was more in the assertion of a right to worship than for the purpose of worshipping, I should still hesitate to hold that the worship was not real, when those engaged in it swear that it was so.

39. The last contention of Mr. Ghose was that, granting that the complainant and his companions were engaged in religious worship, and granting that they were voluntarily disturbed by the accused, it is not shewn that, they were lawfully engaged in such worship, and that the disturbance does not therefore constitute an offence under Section 296 of the Indian Penal Code. I am clearly of opinion that his contention is sound. To sustain a charge under Section 296, it lies upon the prosecution to show that the persons who wore disturbed in their religious worship or ceremonies

were lawfully engaged in the performance of the same, that is, that they had the right to do what they were doing. But the prosecution has utterly failed to discharge the burden of proof that lay upon it. What the complainant and his associates were engaged in doing, was not simply to worship in the upper chamber of the temple, but to enshrine a new image of Buddha on the altar of that chamber, and that, after the refusal of the Mahant, in whose possession and under whose control the temple was, to allow such enshrinement, as shown by the events of May 1894, and without any further intimation to him. It is evident, too, from the previous acts and conduct of the complainant himself, reluctantly admitted by him in his cross-examination, that his object on this occasion was not simply to worship in the temple, but to assert his right to worship there in a particular way, that is, to enshrine the image there in disregard of the authority of the Mahant or, to put it in the mild language of the learned Sessions Judge, "to gain a spiritual triumph for Buddhism, and-to get rid of a responsibility which, although he had sought it himself in the greatest hope and confidence, he now felt was an intolerable burden." In other words, he wanted indirectly and in a covert way to do that which he had failed to do directly and openly, namely, to bring the temple under the control of Buddhist priests.

40. Now, though the Buddhists may have the right to worship in the temple, there is no evidence to shew that they have any right to resort to the temple to secure such an object as the one referred to above, or to enshrine a new image in the temple against the wish, and in the face of the express prohibition, of the Mahant. The learned Sessions Judge, in his judgment, takes exception to the word "enshrinement," but that is the word used in the charge to which the accused were called upon to answer, and that is the word used by the complainant himself with reference to the placing of the Japanese image in the temple. His intention evidently was to place the image in the temple as a permanent object of worship, and he has adduced no evidence to show that he had the right to do so. That being so, it cannot be said that in doing what he did, he was lawfully engaged in religious worship or religious ceremonies. The learned Advocate-General, no doubt, felt the difficulty of the position, and the way in which he sought to get over the difficulty was by arguing that, even if the Mahant had the right to prevent the setting up of the new image, his subordinates, the accused, were at best entitled to stop the placing of the image on the altar before the commencement of the worship, or to remove it after the conclusion of the same, but they were not justified in disturbing the worship during its continuance. To this argument there are two answers: In the first place, however desirable it

may be, that religious worship from its sacred character should, while it is going on, be secured against molestation, even though the worshipper be a wrong-doer and a trespasser, that is not provided for by our criminal law, and the Legislature has thought it fit to make molestation of religious worship an offence only when people are lawfully engaged in their worship. And in the second place, upon the admitted facts of the case, the opposition effectually began before the worship had commenced and the lighting of the candles, which is regarded as a necessary preliminary, had taken place, and the subsequent removal of the image was only a continuation of the first opposition.

41. I, therefore, think that it is not established that the complainant and his associates were lawfully engaged in religious worship, when they were disturbed, and that the accused, therefore, in causing the disturbance have committed no offence under Section 296 of the Indian Penal Code; and I agree with my learned colleague in holding that this rule should be made absolute, the convictions and sentences set aside, and the fines, if realised, refunded.

Appendix 4

1949 BODHGAYA TEMPLE ACT

THE BODHGAYA TEMPLE ACT, 1949

(THE BODHGAYA TEMPLE ACT, 1949 17 OF 1949)

(as modified up to the 8th February, 1955)

[Governor's assent published in the Bihar Gazette of the 6th July, 1949].

An Act to make provision for the better management of the Bodh Gaya Temple and the properties appertaining thereto.

Whereas it is expedient to make provision for the better management of the Bodh Gaya Temple and properties appertaining thereto.

It is hereby enacted as follows:-

Short little and Commencement

1. (I) This Act may be called the Bodh Gaya Temple Act, 1949.

(II) It shall come into force at once.

Definition

2. In this Act, unless there is any thing repugnant in the subject or context-

(a) "the temple" means the great temple built by the site of the Mahabodhi Tree near the village ofBodh Gaya in the district of Gaya and includes the Mahabodhi Tree and Vajrasan;

(b) "the temple land" means the land in which the temple and its precincts stand and shall cover such area or shall lie within such boundaries as the [2] [State] Government may, by notification direct;

(c) "the Mahanth" means the presiding priest for the time being of Saivite Monastery at Bodh Gaya; and

(d) "Committee" means the committee constituted under Section 3.

3. (1) As soon as may be after the commencement of this the 1 [State] Government shall constitute a committee as hereinafter provided and entrust it with the management and control of the temple land and the properties appeartaining thereto.

(2) The Committee shall consist of a Chairman and eight members nominated by the [1] [State] Government, all of whom shall be Indians and of whom four shall be Buddhists and four shall be Hindus including the Mahanth:

Provided that if the Mahanth is a minor or of unsound mind or refuses to serve on the committee, another Hindu member shall be nominated in his place.

(3) The District Magistrate of Gaya shall be the ex-officio Chairman of the Committee: Provided that the 1 [State] Government shall nominate a Hindu as Chairman of the Committee for the period during which the district Magistrate of Gaya is non-Hindu.

(4) The [1] [State] Government shall nominate a person from among the members to act as Secretary of the Committee.

4. The Committee shall be a body corporate by the name of the Bodh Gaya Temple Management Committee, having perpetual succession and a common seal, with power to acquire and hold property, both movable and immovable, and to contract, and shall by the said name sue or be sued.

5. (1) The term of office of the members of the committee shall be three years:

Provided that the 1 [State] Government, if they are satisfied that the Committee is guilty of gross mismanagement, dissolve the Committee and constitute another Committee or assume direct control of the temple, temple land and the properties appertaining thereto.

(2) Where a member of the Committee dies, resigns, refuses to serve on the Committee, absents himself from six consecutive meetings of the Committee, without the leave of the Committee or ceases to reside in India, or becomes in capable of working, the [1] [State] Government may nominate a person to fill the vacancy.

(3) Any Act done by the Committee shall not be questioned on the ground merely of the existence of any vacancy in or any defect in the constitution of the Committee.

6. The name of the Chairman other than the District Magistrate of Gaya and of every member of the committee shall be published by the 1 [State] Government in the Official Gazzette,

7. (1) The Committee shall maintain its office at Bodh Gaya.

(2) At the meeting of the Committee the Chairman, or in his absence one of the members to be elected at the meeting, shall preside.

(3) No business shall be transacted at any meeting unless at least four members are present.

8. (1) No movable property of a non-perish able nature appertaining to the temple shall be transferred without the previous sanction of the Committee, and, if the value of the property is more than one thousand rupees, without the previous approval of the 1 [State] Government.

(2) No immovable property appertaining to the temple shall be leased for more than three years or mortgaged, sold or otherwise alienated except with the previous sanction of the committee and the [1] [State] Government.

9. The Committee shall have no proper to borrow money from any person except with the previous sanction of the 1 [State] Government.

10. Subject to the provisions of this Act or of any rules made there under, it shall be the duty of the Committee-

(1) to arrange for

(a) the upkeep and repair of the temple;

(b) the improvement of the temple land;

(c) the welfare and safety of the pilgrims; and

(d) the proper performance of worship at the temple and pindadan (offering of pindas) on the temple land;

(2) to prevent the descration of the temple or any part thereof or of any image therein;

(3) to make arrangements for the receipt and disposal of the offerings made in the Temple, and for the safe custody of the statements of accounts and other documents relating to the temple or the temple land and for the preservation of the property appertaining to the temple;

(4) to make arrangement for the custody, deposit and investment of funds in its hand; and

(5) to make provision for the payment of suitable emoluments to its salaried staff.

11. (1) Notwithstanding anything contained in this Act or in the rules framed there under, Hindus and Buddhists of every sect shall have access to the temple and the temple land for the purpose of worship or pindadan.

Provide that nothing in this Act shall entitle any person to perform animal sacrifice or to bring any alcoholic liqueur within the temple or on the temple land, or to enter the temple with shoes on.

(2) If any person contravenes the provisions of the proviso to sub-Section (1), he shall be punishable with fine not exceeding fifty rupees.

12. Notwithstanding anything contained in any enactment for the time being in force, if there be any dispute between Hindus and Buddhists regarding the manner of using the temple or the temple land, the decision of the 1 [State] Government shall be final.

13. Notwithstanding anything contained in this Act or in the rules made there under, the Committee shall have no jurisdiction over the movable or immovable property of the Saivite Monastery of Bodh Gaya.

14. The 1 [State] Government shall every year appoint on auditor to audit the accounts of the funds of the Committee and fix his remuneration which shall be paid from the said funds. The auditor shall submit his report to the Committee and send a copy of if to the [1] [State] Government which may issue such directions thereon, as it may deem fit, and the Committee shall carry out such directions.

15. (1) The 1 [State] Government may constitute an Advisory Board (hereinafter

referred to in this Act as the "Board") which shall consist of such number of members as the [1] [State] Government may determine.

(2) The majority of the members of such Board shall be Buddhists who may not all be Indians.

(3) The members of the Board shall hold office for such term as may be fixed by the [1] [State] Government.

(4) The Board shall function purely as an Advisory body to the Committee and shall discharge its furctious in the .... prescribed by the 1 [State] Government by rules made...... behalf.

16. This Act shall have effect notwithstanding anything to the contrary contained in the Religious endowments Act 2 1863, or in any decree, custom or usage.

17. (1) With the previous sanction of he 3 [State] Government the committee may, from time, make bye-laws to carry out the purposes of this Act.

(2) In particular, and without prejudice to the generality of the foregoing powers, such byelaws may provide for:-

(a) the division of duties among the Chair-, man, the members and Secretary of the Committee;

(b) the manner in which their decision may be ascertained otherwise than at the meetings;

(c) the procedure and conduct of business at meetings of the Committee;

(d) the delegation of powers of the Committee to individual members;

(e) the book and accounts to be kept at the office of the Committee;

(f) the custody and investment of the dunds of the Committee;

(g) the time and place of its meetings;

(h) the manner in which notice of its meeting shall be given;

(i) the preservation of order and the conduct of proceeding at meetings and the powers which the Chairman may exercise for the purpose of enforcing its decisions;

(j) the manner in which the proceeding of its meeting shall be recorded;

(k) the persons by whom receipts may be granted for moneys paid to the Committee; and

(l) the maintenance of cordial relations between the Buddhists and the Hindu pilgrims.

(3) All bye-laws, after they have been confirmed by the 1 [State] Government, shall be published in the Official Gazette, and shall thereafter have the force of law.

18. The 1 [State] Government may make rules 2 to carry out the purposes of this Act.

[Preface to the said Act: "The Bodh Gaya Temple Act, 1949 (Bihar Act 17 of 1949) has been amended by the Adaptation of Law Order, 1950. The amendments made by the Adaptation of Laws Order have been incorporated in the text and some other foot-notes have been added for convenience of reference"—Deputy Secretary to Government, dated the 8th February, 1955].3

BYE-LAWS OF THE BODH GAYA TEMPLE MANAGEMENT COMMITTEE

Government of Bihar, Political Department. (General Branch) NOTIFICATION.

Patna, the 26th February, 1957

No. A/B1-1026/56-P.G. 435. The following bye-laws made by the Bodh Gaya Temple Management Committee under Sub-section (1) of Section 17 of the Bodh Gaya Temple Act, 1949 (Bihar Act 17 of 1949), having been confirmed by the State Government, are hereby published as required by Sub-section (3) of the said Section:-

By-laws under Section 17 of the Bodh Gaya Temple Act.

1. In these bye-laws unless the context otherwise indicates:

(i) 'Act means the Bodh Gaya Temple Act, 1949 (Bihar Act XVIII of 1949).

(ii) 'rules' means rules farmed by the State Government under section 18 of the Act.

(iii) 'Bye-laws' means the bye-laws framed by the Committee with the previous sanction of the State Government under section 17 of the Act.

(iv) 'Chairman' means the Chairman of the Committee.

(v) 'Secretary' means the Secretary of the Committee.

2. Meetings of the Committee shall be hels at the office of the Committee or at such other place at Bodh Gaya as the Chairman or in his absence, the Secretary may decide.

3. Meetings of the Committee shall be held, as far as possible, at intervals to exceeding three months.

4. The agenda for a meeting shall be prepared by the Chairman after taking into consideration suggestions (if any) received in this behalf from the members, and resolutions received in the office of the Committee at least seven days before the notice meeting is issued to members shall be included therein.

5. Notice of a meeting together with copies of the agenda shall be circulated to members by post by Express delivery letters, or by messengers i case of local members, at least, twenty-one days before the date fixed for the meeting Providing that in case of an emergency a meeting may be called on seven days' notice.

6. Notice of a meeting together with the agenda shall be entered in a register kept for the purpose, and the register shall be open to inspection by any member at the office of the Committee during office hours.

7. The Chairman (or, in his absence, any other member elected for the purpose by members present at the meeting) shall preside over a meeting.

8. Four members shall form the quorum at any meeting.

9. The minutes of proceedings of meetings shall be recorded by the Chairman, or, in his absence, by the member who may preside at the meeting or by such other person as may be directed by the person presiding at the meeting.

10. At a meeting other than an adjourned meeting, the minutes of the last meeting shall be read out and, if approved as having been correctly recorded or after necessary correction, if any, shall be signed by the Chairman or such other member as may be presiding at the meeting.

11. At every meeting a financial statement and a report on the work done after the last meeting of the committee (including a resume of the steps taken to implement the previous decisions of the Committee), or proposed to be undertaken in future, shall be laid.

12. No subject once finally disposed of at a meeting shall be reopened or reconsidered within six months from the date of its disposal, except with the concurrence of, at least, two-thirds of the members present at a meeting.

13. The Chairman may issue special invitations to persons who are not members of the Committee to attend a meeting and the invitees may participate in the deliberations of the Committee, but they will have no right of vote.

15. An adjourned meeting, being merely continuation of the original meeting, shall not require notice of more than seven days.

16. No matter may be considered at a meeting including a meeting adjourned for want of the quorum unless it is included in the agenda circulated under bye-law 5:

Provided that, at the request of any member or on his motion, the Chairman (or, in his absence, the member presiding at the meeting) may include any matter in the agenda if he is satisfied about its urgency.

17. Any member of the Committee may make suggestions in writing for the inclusion of any matter in the agenda of a meeting and the same shall be considered by the Chairman and, in case the Chairman does not include in the agenda any such suggestion which has been received in the office of the Committee more than seven days before the notice together with the agenda is issued to the members, he shall record the reasons for inability to include the suggestion in the agenda and inform the member concerned of it.

18. The suggestions mentioned in bye-law No. 18 shall together with the date of their receipt in the office of the Committee be entered in the order in which they are received in a register to be maintained for the purpose.

19. The Chairman, or the Secretary, in consultation with the Chairman, shall

convene meetings of the Committee;

Provide that, if no meeting is held within three months, any member may send a requisition to the Chairman requesting him to call a meeting and the Chairman (or the Secretary in consultation with the Chairman) shall thereupon call a meeting of the Committee and, if the Chairman (or the Secretary) fails to call a meeting within a year, any four members may call a meeting of the Committee.

20. Within seven days of the holding of a meeting, the minutes of the proceedings of the meeting shall be circulated to all members of the Committee, and a copy thereof shall be forwarded to the State Government and the Commissioner, Patna Division by the Chairman.

21. (i) If any question of importance requiring urgent consideration arises, the Secretary, with the consent of the Chairman, or the Chairman on his own motion may ascertain the opinions of the members thereon otherwise than at a meeting by referring the matter to them in writing by registered post.

(ii) In making the reference the question on which the opinion of the members is to be ascertained shall, as far as practicable, be framed succinctly and precisely, split into parts, if necessary, so that the answer to the parts or whole may be 'yes' or 'no'.

(iii) A short explanation note shall accompany the question.

(iv) The decision of the majority of the members so ascertained shall operate as the decision of the Committee and shall have the same binding force and effect as that of a decision arrived at a meeting.

(v) The majority opinion shall be calculated and determined on the basis of opinions received in the office of the Committee before the 22nd day of the despatch of the registered letters in this regard to the members:

Provided that, if the majority opinion becomes clear before the lapse of the said period of 21 days, the Secretary shall proceed to act on it forthwith.

(iv) The opinion so ascertained shall be reported in writing to the next meeting of the Committee and then incorporated in its minutes.

22. The annual budget of the Committee shall be finalised every year not later than the 31st January, and, at least, one month before the date of the meeting

convened for the purpose of considering and passing the budget, the Secretary shall, in consultation with the Chairman, prepare:-

(i) an estimated budget of expenditure which may be incurred during the ensuing financial year;

(ii) a statement showing all expected receipts from all sources during the ensuing financial year;

(iii) an estimate of the balances likely to be available for expenditure during the ensuing financial year, and circulate them with an explanatory memorandum, to all members of the committee at least 21 days before the date of the meeting.

23. No expenditure shall be incurred unless it is sanctioned in the budget:

Provided that, to meet unforeseen and urgent expenditure, the Committee shall, subject to rules, be competent to sanction special grants during the year.

24. The power of the Committee to sanction special grants to meet unforeseen and urgent expenditure, may by a resolution of the Committee, be delegated to the Chairman and/or the Secretary.

25. At the meeting of the Committee convened to consider the annual budget estimates, statements and proposals, the Secretary shall place the final accounts of the financial year next preceding and the provisional accounts of the financial year.

26. The budget for a financial year passing at the meeting of the Committee referred to in the bye-law 23, shall be forwarded for information to the State Government, and to such other authority as the State Government may, from time to time, indicae,

27. All money received whether by way of donation, subscription or any other manner, shall be credited to the Fund of the Committee.

28. Charity boxes shall be opened at least a month by the Chairman or any other person authorised by him in writing, in presence of two other responsible persons who will each certify in writing what amount is taken out of each such box.

29. Accounts will be maintained in the local branch of the State Bank of India.

30. All money received by or on behalf of the Committee must be deposited in the Bank within the next three working days of the bank after such receipt.

31. Payments exceeding Rs. 20.00 except the payment of salaries and emoluments of the staff of the Committee, shall be made by cheques signed by the Chairman or signed by the Secretary and countersigned by the Chairman.

32. For all money any articles received by or on behalf of the Committee the Chairman or any other person authorised in writing by him shall issue printed receipts, the counterfoils of which shall be preserved for a period of twelve years.

33. The income and the property of the Committee, howsoever derived, shall be applied solely towards the proper performance of the duties of the Committee as laid down in the Act.

34. Subject to the control of the Chairman, the Secretary shall be in charge of the funds of the committee.

35. Subject to the provisions of the Act all transfer of properties, movable or immovable, whether by way of lease, mortgage, sale or otherwise shall be openly negotiated and completed:

Provided that the Chairman, or such person as may be authorised in writing by him in this behalf, may have any perishable article auctioned after giving locally notice of the auction by beat of drum.

36. All leases and contracts shall be made in open public bids held after seven days of proper and public notice.

37. The lease shall usually be given to the highest bidder for reasons to be recorded in writing by him.

38. In giving out contracts, the lowest tender shall ordinarily be accepted:

Provided that the Chairman will have the right to give a contract to a person whose tender is not the lowest for reasons to be recorded in writing by him.

39. The Chairman may authorise the Secretary or the senior most member of

the staff of the Committee to keep with himself a permanent advance of a sum not exceeding Rs.50/- for incurring expenditure on contingencies, which will be recouped by drawing regular bills after submission of proper vouchers for each item of expenditure already incurred.

41. (i) The appointment or the dismissal of member of the staff of the Committee employed on a salary of Rs. 50/- a month and above shall rest with the Committee.

(ii) The Chairman may appoint, suspend or dismiss any employee of the Committee whose salary is less than Rs. 50/- a month:

Provided that, all such appointments, suspensions and dismissals must be reported with the reasons therefore for information at the first meeting of the Committee held after the order or appointment, suspension or dismissal has been passed.

(iii) The Chairman may, pending an inquiry, suspend an employee of the committee drawing a salary of Rs. 50/- a month or more for misconduct, incompetence, neglect of duty or any other sufficient cause:

Provided that he action taken along with the explanation, if any, submitted by the employee, shall be reported to the Committee for proper action all its first meeting held after the order of suspension has been passed.

(iv) All temporary employees of the Committee, whose services may no longer by required hall be liable to be discharged after one month's notice or on payment of one month's salary in lieu thereof. Permanent employees may be removed from service after consideration of an explanation to be submitted by them within a reasonale time.

(v) The Chairman may impose a fine not exceeding one tenth of one month's salary on any employee of the Committee drawing a salary not exceeding Rs. 50/- a month for misconduct, neglect of duty or any other sufficient cause.

(vi) The Chairman may impose a fine not exceeding one-tenth of one month's salary on any employees of the committee drawing a salary of Rs. 50/- a month or above but the order imposing the fine shall be submitted to the Committee for approval at its first meeting held after the order is passed and the Committee may approve, rescind, or modify the order.

(vii) The Chairman shall call upon the employee concerned to explain his conduct and consider the explanation, if any, submitted by the employee before he passes an order imposing a fine.

(viii) All persons employed by a Committee shall, if required, furnish such security as the Committee may from time to time determine.

(ix) During the period of suspension pending enquiry into his conduct, an employee will get as subsistence allowance only one-half of the salary which he was entitled to draw on the day he was suspended.

42. The General superintendence and control of the establishments maintained by the Committee shall vest in and be exercised by the Chairman. The Chairman shall be in general control of the funds of the Committee and shall enter into contracts or execute leases or other documents and pass bills for payments, on behalf of the committee.

43. The Secretary shall be the Chief Executive Officer of the Committee, and shall excericse supervision over the staff of the committee and keep the books of accounts and other principal records of the Committee.

43. The Secretary shall be the chief Executive Officer of the Committee, and shall excericse supervision over the staff of the Committee and keep the books of accounts and other principal records of the Committee in his custody.

44. The Committee may designate the senior most member of its office staff as its Superintendent who shall:-

(i) have the general charge of the office of the Committee and its day to day work

(ii) subject to any general or special direction which the Chairman or Secretary may from time to time give, deal with routine correspondence.

(iii) examine and sign the cash-books and keep them in order and up-to-date;

(iv) he responsible for the maintenance of the purity and cleanliness of the Temple and the Temple land; and.

(v) look after the comforts of visitors and devotees.

45. All communication received in the office marked 'Secret', 'Confidential',

or 'Personal', (or addressed by name) shall be opened by the Chairman or the Secretary (according as who is the addressee).

46. The common seal of the Committee shall remain in the custody of the Chairman, or, if he so directs in writing, of the Secretary.

47. The common seal shall be affixed to the following documents:-

(i) all deeds of transfer executed by, or, on behalf of the Committee;

(ii) all written contracts entered into by the Committee;

(iii) the minutes of proceedings of the Committee;

(iv) notices of the meetings of the Committee;

(v) all receipts for money grated on behalf of the Committee; and

(vi) any other documents which in the opinion of the Chairman or the Secretary, is of importance

48. (i) For the proper maintenance of accounts and efficient discharge of its duties the Committee shall maintain necessary books and registers in its office.

(ii) A list of such books and registers shall be maintained in the office

(iii) Books and registers maintained by the Committee shall be open to inspection, during office hours, by the members of the committee and with the permission of the Chairman or the Secretary, by any other person.

49. The Committee may from time to time, for any purpose connected with its work, appoint sub-committees consisting of such of its members and any others persons as it may think proper and such sub-committees shall exercise such powers and perform such functions as may be prescribed by the Committee.

50. Any addition, alteration or modification in these bye-laws may be made by the Committee by a majority of votes of the members of the Committee, subject to confirmation by the State Government and publication in the official Gazette.

51. In matters no specifically provided for in these by-laws the Committee shall be competent to pass orders and regulate its affairs in such manner as in necessary for the discharge of its duties in accordance with the Act and the rules.

52. The Committee may, by a resolution, delegate such of its powers to the Chairman or the Secretary as it may consider necessary.

53. The Secretary shall prepare each year a report of the affairs and activities of the committee and present it at its meeting held to consider and pass the budget. A copy of the report shall be forwarded to the State Government along with the budget estimates.

54. The members of the Committee including the Chairman and the Secretary and the special invitees to the meetings of the Committee and Sub-committees shall be entitled to travelling allowance and daily allowance for attending the meetings of the Committee and its Sub-committees (and for other journeys required in connection with the work of the Committee, in the case of the Chairman and Secretary) at the following rates:

(i) Single second class railway fare from the railway station nearest the members or special invitees, place or residence to the railway stations nearest the place of the meeting.

(ii) Eight annas for each mile of distance travelled by road in the course of journey from the place of residence to the place of meeting.

(iii) Daily allowance at the rate of Rs. 5/- per diem for the duration of the meeting and an allowance of Rs. 5/- as out of pocket expenses for every day spent in travelling between their places of residence and the place of the meeting and vice versa:

Provided that, the out-of-pocket expenses shall not be paid for the day or days for which daily allowance is admissible.

Provided further that, that employees of the State Government shall not be entitled to charge any travelling allowance or daily allowance or out-of-poket expense from the funds of the Committee.

55. The staff of the Committee shall be entitled to such rates of travelling and daily allowances as the Chairman may, from time to time, after due consideration of the finances of the Committee, by an order in writing determine and

such rates shall until modified.

Bibliography

1. Literatures in English

Ahir, D.C. *Buddha Gaya Through the Ages*. Sri Satguru Publications. Delhi. 1994 p.190.

———. *Buddhism Declined in India, How and Why*. B.R. Publishing. Delhi. 2005.

Almond, P.C. *The British Discovery of Buddhism*. Cambridge University Press. 1988.

Anuruddha, D.N. (Ed). *The Crisis of Secularism in India*, Duke University Press Books. 2006. Rep. 2007.

Asher, F.M. *Bodh Gaya Monumental Legacy*. Oxford University Press. New Delhi. 2008. p. 98.

Bahadur, R.R.A.N.S. Under the order of G.A. Grierson. *A Brief History of Bodh Gaya Math, District Gaya*. The Bengal Secretariat Press. 1893.

Barua, B. Gaya and Buddha Gaya. *Early History of the Holy Land*. 2 Vols. Calcutta. 1931–1934. (Rep.) 1975.

Barua, D.K. *Buddha Gaya Temple, it's History*. "Prajna" Buddhagaya Temple Management Commtee.

———. *Buddha Gaya Temple, it's History*. Buddha-Gaya Temple Mamagement Committee. 1981. 320p.

Bauddh, S.S. Bodhgaya. *The Great Sacred Place of Buddhists*. Buddhist Ideals series. Samyak Prakashan. New Delhi. 2005. 128p.

———. *In the Foot Steps of The Buddha: Eight Buddhist Shrines in India*. Samyak Prakashan.

Beal, S. *The Chinese Buddhist Inscription found at Buddha Gaya. No 1. Chinese*. JRAS Vol. 13, 1881. 69p. Plate pp. 552–572 London.

———. Indian Travels of Chinese Buddhist. *Indian Antiquary. Vol. 10*. 1881. pp. 109–111, 192–197, 246–248.

———. *Si-Yu-Ki Buddhist Records of the Western World*. (Rep.) Oriental Book Reprint Corporation. Delhi. 1961.

Block, T. Notes on Bodh Gaya. (In) *Annual Report 1908–9 of the Archaeological Survey of India*. Superintendant, Government Printing. 1912 pp. 139–158.

(The) Bodhgaya Temple Act, 1949 17 of 1949. *Bihar Gazette* of the 6th July 1949. Patna. 15p.

Bodh–Gaya Marga. Bombay. 1988. 155p.
Introduction.
Leoshko, J.

The Mahabodhi Temple.
Malandra, G.H.
The Vjrasana Buddha.
Leoshko, J.
Votive Objects from Bodhgaya.
Lawson, S.
Gaya: Monuments of the Pilgrimage Town.
Asher, F.M.
Bodhgaya and Sri Lanka.
Dehejia, V.
Bodhgaya and South-east Asia.
Brown, R.L.
Bodhgaya and Nepal.
Slussen, M.S.
Bodhgaya and Tibet.
Singer, J.C.

Buchanan (Hamilton), F. *An Account of the District of Bihar and Patna in 1811–1812*. (Ed.) with Notes and Introduction by V.H. Jackson. Superintendent, Government Printing, Behar and Orissa. Patna. 1925. 250p. (Rep.) Usha. New Delhi. 1986. 399p.

———. *Journal of Francis Buchanan 1811–1812*. (Ed.) V.H.Jackson. Asian Educational Services. New Delhi. 1989. 250p.

Buddhist legend concerning the site of Mahabodhi Temple. (Logemy, Downroaded on March 24. 2013.)

Chakravarty, K.K. *Early Buddhist Art of Bodh-Gaya*. Munsiram Manoharlal Publishers. New Delhi. 1997. 70p.

Chakravarty, S. *Antiquities from Bodhgaya in the Indian Museum*. !Prajna! Bodhgaya Temple Manegement committee. 2006. Pp. 63–66.

Chaudhry, S.K. *Buddhist Denied Justice: The law and the Mahabodhi at Bodh-Gaya*. 2011. Countercurrents.org

Cunningham, A. *Mahabodhi. The Great Buddhist Temple*. W.H. & Co. London. Rep. Munsiram Manoharlal Publishers. New Delhi. 1998.

Curzon, G.N. *Bodh Gaya*. (In) proceedings of the Home Department. 7. Public Deposit. 3. National Archaives of India. 1902. pp. 218–337. Indian Kanoon org/doc/1821. 486.

Curson Collection. *Indian Archaelogy 1899–1905, in the India Office Records of the India Office Library*. London.

David, S. *Buddhism and Islam: Past to Present Encounter and Interfaith Lessons*. Numen. 42 (2) pp. 141–151. 1995. http;//www.jstor.org

Denyer, S. Scandal gnaws at Buddhist's Holy Tree in India. *The Buddhist Channel*. 2008. February 3.

Department of Urban Development, Gov't. of Bihar. *City Development Plan revised Final Report.* (Revised November .2006) Consultant: Housing and Urban Development Corporation LTD. New Delhi. 2006. 232p.

Dharmapala, A. *Letter dated 7, Feburary to The Home Department. (In) Proceedings of the Home Department, Nos 466/69. 1901. Public B 1904.*

(The) Education of Bodaiju Gakuen. International Brotherhood Association. Tokyo. 2008. 51p.

Excavation at Taradih Gaya. *Indian Archaeology a Rewiew.* 1981–82, 1982–83, 1983–84, 1984-85, 1985–86, 1986–87, 1987–88, 1988–89. Archaelogical Survey of India New Delhi.

Frederic, M.A. *Bodhgaya.* Oxford University Press, New Delhi. 2008.

Gaya District. *Imperial Gazetter of India Vol. xii.* Oxford Claredon Press. 1908. Gaya Dist. p.194–, Gaya Town p. 208, Vol. ix p. 43.

(Ed.) Geary, D., Sayers, M.R. and Amar, A.S. Cross-disciplinary perspectives on a Contested Buddhist Site. *Bodh Gaya Jataka.* Routradge. London. 2012.

Getty, A. *The God of Northern Buddhism.* Oxford Clarendon Press. 1914.

Goodearth, E. *Walking with The Buddha, Buddhist Pilgrimages in India.* New Delhi. 1999. 2004. 2009. 2012. 192p.

Guy, J. *The Mahabodhi Temple: Pilgrim Souvenirs of Buddhist India.* The Burlington Magazine. 133. No. 1059. 1991. pp. 356–368.

Hoey, W. Extract from the Commissioner, Gorakhpur Division, to the Chief Secretary to the Government of the North-Western Provinces and Oudh. (In) Proceedings of the Home Department. Nos. 3-20. Public-A: 12–14. 1899b.

———. Address by the Commissioner, Gorakhpur Division, to the Royal Commissioner of Siam. (In) Proceedings of the Home Department. Nos. 3–20. Pubic-A: 14–15. 1899a.

Huntington, S.L., Huntington, J.C. Leaves from the Bodhi Tree: The Art of Pala India (8th–12th Centuries) and Its International Legacy. *Orientations.* Vol. 20. No. 10. Hong Kong. 1989. pp. 2–22.

(Tr.) Jacques, C. *Gaya Mahatmya.* Institut Francais d!Indlogie Pondichery. 1962. 428p.

(Tr.) Jan Yun-Hua. *A Chronicle of Buddhism in China. 581–960 A.D.* Visva-Bharati Santiniketan. 1966. 189p.

Kinnard, J.N. When is the Buddha Not the Buddha. The Hindu/Buddhist Battle Over Buddhagaya and its Buddha Image. *Journal of the American Academy of Religion.* Vol. 64. No 4. 1998. pp. 817–839.

Lahiri, N. Bodh-Gaya: an Ancient Buddhist Shrine and its Modern History. (1891–1904) Department of History, University of Delhi. (In) Case Studied in Archaeology and World Religions, The Proceedings of the Cambridge Conference. (Ed.) Timothy Insoll. pp. 33–43. BAR International Series

755. Oxford. 1999.

Law, B.C. Bodh Gaya. *Historical Geography of Ancient India.* Societe Asiatique de Paris. Paris. 1954. 213p.

Leoshko, J. *Iconography of Buddhist Sculputuers of the Pala and Sena Periods from Bodhgaya.* PhD. Dissertation, The Ohio State University. 1987.

———. The Significance of Bodhgaya's Surya. (In) *Aksayanivi: Essays Presented to Debala Mitra in Admiration to the Scholarly Contributions.* (Ed.) G. Bhattacariya. Sri Satguru Publications. Delhi. 1991. pp. 185–189.

———. Pilgrimage and the Evidence of Bodhgaya's Images. (In) *Function and Meaning in Buddhist Art.* Proceedings of a Seminar held at Leiden University. 21-24, October. 1991. (Ed.) K.R. van Kooij & H. van der Veer. Egbert Farstern, Groningen. 1995. pp. 45–57.

———. On the Construction of a Buddhist Pilgrimage Site. *Art History.* Vol. 19 No 4. 1996. pp. 573–597.

———. The Significance of Bodh Gaya. (In) Pilgrimage and Buddhist Art. (Ed.) Adrina Proser. Asia Society, Yale University Press. New Haven and London. 2010.

Liberate the Mahabodhi Temple. Socially Engaged Buddhism. (In) *Buddhism in the Modern World.* (Ed.) Steven Heine and Charles Prebish. Oxford University Press. 2003. pp. 249–280.

Losty, J.R. The Mahabodhi Temple. Before its Restoration. (In) *Aksyavini: Essays Presented to D. Mitra in Admiration of her Scholarly Contributions.* Sri Satguru Publications. Delhi. 1991. pp. 235–267.

Macpherson, Banerjee. *Jaipal Gir and Ors. Vs H. Dhammapala on 22 August, 1895.* Equivalent citations ILR 23 Cal. 60. Judgement. (Indiankanoon. org/doc/1821486/).

Madhukar, K.H., Sahay, B.B. *Bodh Gaya. The Holy Pilgrimage of Buddhists.* Buddhist Center for Action Research and Development Studies. Patna. 1998. 131p.

Mahabodhi Temple. Wikipedia.

Mahabodhi (Mahavihara) Temple. A World Heritage Property. Bodhgaya Temple Management Committee. Bodhgaya. n.d. 37p.

(The) Mahabodhi Temple: Pilgrim Souvenirs of Buddhist India. The Burlington Magazine. Vol. 133, No 1059 1991. pp. 356–367.

Ministry of Tourism, Govt. of India. Heritage Led Perspective Development Plan for Bodhgaya, Vision 2005–2031. Draft Report May 2006. 76p.

Martin, Montogomery. *History, Antiquities, Topography and Statistics of Eastern India, Comprising the District of Behar, Shahabad, Bhagulpoor, Dinajepour, Rungpoor &Assam.* Vol. I. London. 1838.

Mitra, R. *Buddha Gaya: The Grest Buddhist Temple. The Heritage of Sakya Muni.* 1878. (Rep.) Indological Book House. Delhi, Varanasi. 1972.

Mitra, D. Two Images of Bodh Gaya. (In) *Essays in Honour of Dr. James O. Hare.* (Ed.) C. Bautze-Pieron, 1990. Sri Satguru Pubication. Delhi. pp. 152–158.

———. Close Religio-Cultural Bond between Bodh Gaya and Sri Lanka. (In) Facts of Indian Civilization. Recent Perspectives. *Essays in Honour of Prof. B.B. Lal.* (Ed.) Jagat Pati Joshi, Aryan Books International. Vol. 11. New Delhi. 1997. pp. 556–569.

Myer, P.R. The great Temple at Bodh-Gaya. *The Art Bulletin.* Vol. XL. No. 4. 1958. pp. 277–298.

Pannasila, B. Return the Mahabodhi Vihara to Buddhist Control and Revise The Buddhagaya Temple Act of 1949. Memorandom given to the Prime Minister of India, Chief Mister of Biha and others. (Unpublished).

Patil, D.R. *Bodh Gaya. The Antiquarian Remains in Bihar.* K.P. Jayaswal Institute. Patna. 1963. pp. 59–70.

Prasad, A.K.. Excavation at Taradhi, Bodh Gaya. (In) *Art and Archaeology of Eastern India.* N. Akthar. Patna Museum. Patna. 1997. pp. 32–50.

Prudence, R.M. The Great Temple at Bodh-Gaya. *The Art Bulletin.* 40 (4) pp. 277–298.

Ray, H.P. *Narrative of Faith: Buddhism and Colonial Archaeology in Monsoon Asia.* Asia Research Institute Working Paper Series No. 99. Center for Historical Studies. Jawahalal Nehru University. New Delhi & Senior Visiting Research Fellow, Asia Research Institute, National University of Singapore. 2007. 42p.

Roerich, G. *Biography of Dharmaswamin, A Tibetan Monk Pilgrim.* K.P. Jayaswal Research Institute. Patna. 1959. 119p.

Rowena, Robinson & Clark. *Religious Conversion of India: Modes, Motivation and Meaning.* Oxford University Press. New Delhi. 2003.

Roy Chaudhury, P.C. *Buddha and Bodh Gaya.* World Fellowship of Buddhist. Bankok. 2518. BE 61p.

Sangharakshita, B. Anagarika Dharmapala. A Biographical Sketch. (In) *Maha Bodhi Society of India Diamond Jubilee Souvenir 1891-1951.* Calcutta. Mahabodhi Society. 1952.

Sanyal, N. A Buddhist Inscription from Bodh-Gaya Reign of Jayaccandradeva. (In) *Indian Historical Quarterly.* Vol. I 1929, pp. 14–30.

Singh, R.P.B. Sacred Geography and Cosmic Geometries: Interfaces in Holy Places of North India. *The Indological Forum.* (Ed.) Calvaruso, D. 2010. www.tirthaplanetindia.org. 20p.

Singh, R.P.B., J.K. Malville, A.L. Marshall. *Sacredscape and Manescape: A Study of Gaya.* (Down Roaded on 2011/11/28) 15p.

Singh, R.P.B. *Where The Buddha Waalked. A Companion to the Buddhist Places of India.* Indica Books. Varanasi. 2003. 330p.

Sircar, D.C. Buddhagaya Stone Slab Inscription of Buddhasena in the Berlin

Museum. *Journal of Ancient Indian History*. Vol. VI, 1972–73. Calcutta. 1973. pp. 47–53.

Srivastava, K.M. The Place of Buddha's Sujata Discovered. *The Journal of the Bihar Puravid Parisad*. Patna. Vol. I. 1977. pp. 133–137.

Sylvan Levi, M.L. Les Missions de Wang Hiuen-Ts'e dans L'Inde. *Journal Asiatique*. Paris. 1900. pp. 297–468.

———. The Mission of Wang Hiuen-Ts'e in India. (Tr.) S.P. Chatterjee. *Bibiotheca Indo Buddhica*. No. 39. Sri Satguru Publications. Delhi. 1967. (Rep.) 1987. 80p.

The Classsical Age. Northern India During A.D. 650–750. (On Wang-Hiuen-tse) (In) *The History and Culture of the Indian People*. (Ed.) K.M.Munshi. Vol.III p. 124–. Bharatiya Vidya Bhavan. Bombay. 1954, (Rep.) 1962.

Trevithick, A. British Archaeologists, Hindu Abbots and Burmese Buddhists. The Mahabodhi Temple at Bodh Gaya 1811–1877. *Modern Asian Studies*. 33 (3) pp. 635–656.

———. *The Revival of Buddhist Pilgrimage at Bodh Gaya. A. Dhammapala and the Mahabodhi Temple*. Motilal Banarsidass Delhi. 2006. 259p.

Valisinha, D. Diary Leaves of the late Ven. Anagarika Dharmapala. *The Mabodhi* 58 (10) pp. 34–35.

Verardi, G. *Hardships and Downfall of Buddhism in India*. Manohar. New Delhi. 2011. 523p.

Visions of Enlightenment, The Heritage of Bodhgaya.

Leoshko, J.L.

Introduction

Malandra, G.H.

The Mahaabodhi Temple.

Leoshko, J.L.

The Vajrasana Buddha

Asher, F.M.

Gaya: Monuments of the Pilgrimage town.

Brown, R.L. Bodhgaya and South-East Asia.

Marga Vol. XXXX No. 1.

Xinru Liu, Chakravarti. A Note on The Chinese Inscription in The Indian Museum. *Indian Museum Bulletin*. Calcutta. 1994. pp. 77–79.

2. Literatures in Chinese

范祥雍. 唐代中印交通吐蕃一道考. 中华文史论丛 第四辑. 上海古籍出版社. 1982. pp. 195–227

(Fan Xiang Yong. Tang dai zhong yin jiao tong tu fan yi dao kao. Zhong hua wen shi lun cong di si ji. Shang hai gu ji chu ban she. 1982. pp.

195–227)
冯承钧. 王玄策事辑. 清华学报. 国立清华大学. 1932. pp. 1–30
(Feng Cheng Diao. Wang xuan ce shi ji. Qing hua xue bao. Guo li qing hua da xue. 1932. pp. 1–30)
冯承钧 撰. 王玄策事辑. 西域南海史地考证论著汇辑. 中华书局 香港分局. 1976. pp. 102–128
(Feng Cheng Jun ji. Wang xuan ce shi ji xi yu nan hai shi di kao zheng lun zhe hui jí. Zhong hua shu ju Xiang gang fen ju. 1976. pp. 102–128)
霍巍. 大唐天竺使出铭及其相关问题的研究. 东京学报 京都第66册. 1994. pp. 270–253
(Huo Wei. Da tang tian zhu shi chu ming ji qi xiang guan wen ti de yan jiu. Dong jing xue bao jing du di 66 ce. 1994. pp. 270–253)
陆庆夫. 关于王玄策史迹研究的几点商权. 兰州大学出版社. 1999. pp. 90–103
(Lu Qing Fu. Guan yu wang xuan ce shi ji yan jiu de ji dian shang quan. Lan zhou da xue Chu ban she. 1999. pp. 90–103)
———. 关于王玄策史迹研究的几点商权. 敦煌研究 第4期 总第46期. 敦煌研究院. 1995
(———. Guan yu wang xuan ce shi ji yan jiu de ji dian shang quan. Dun huang yan jiu Di 4 ji Zong di 46 qi. Dun huang yan jiu yuan. 1995)
———. 论王玄策对中印交通的贡献. 敦煌学辑刊. 1984. pp. 100–109
(———. Lun wang xuan ce dui zhong yin jiao tong de gong xian. Dun huang xue ji kan. 1984. pp. 100–109)
———. 论王玄策对中印交通的贡献. 丝绸之路史地研究. 兰州大学出版社. 1999. pp. 71–89
(———. Lun wang xuan ce dui zhong yin jiao tong de gong xian. Si chou zhi lu shi di yan jiu. Lan zhou da xue chu ban she. 1999. pp. 71–89)
孙修身. 王玄策事迹钩沉. 西域佛教研究丛书. 新疆人民出版社. 1998. pp. 281
(Sun Xiu Shen. Wang xuan ce shi ji gou chen. Xi yu fo jiao yan jiu cong shu. Xin jiang ren min chu ban she. 1998. pp. 281)
郑炳林 魏迎春. 俄藏敦煌写本王玄策《中天竺国行记》残卷考释. 敦煌学辑刊. 2005. pp. 3–11
(Zheng Fan Lin Wei Ying Chun. E cang dun huang xie ben wang xuan ce 'zhong tian zhu guo xing ji can juan kao shi. Dun huang xue ji kan. 2005. pp. 3–11)
册府元龟
(Ce fu yuan gui)
大慈恩寺三藏法师传
(Da ci en si san zang fa shi zhuan)
大唐西域记
(Da tang xi yu ji)
大唐西域求法高僧传
(Da tang xi yu qiu fa gao seng zhuan)

读高僧传
(Du gao seng zhuan)
法显传
(Fa xian zhuan)
法苑珠林
(Fa yuan zhu lin)
佛祖说记
(Fo zu shuo ji)
旧唐书
(Jiu tang shu)
释迦方志
(Shi jia fang zhi)
新唐书
(Xin tang shu)
资治通鉴
(Zi zhi tong jian)

3. Literatures in Japanese

天沼俊一（Amanuma, Syunichi）印度仏塔巡礼記。上、下。秋田屋。大阪。昭和十八年。399頁、図版320頁。（Pilgrimage to the Buddhist Stupa in India.）

石井公成（Ishii, Kouichi）明治期における海外渡航僧の諸相。北畠道竜、小泉了諦、織田得能、井上秀夫、A. ダルマパーラ。近代仏教第十五号。東京。2008。（Japanese Buddhist abroad in Meiji Era.）

尾高鮮之助（Odaka, Sennosuke）印度日記。仏教美術の源流を訪ねて。刀江書院。東京。昭和十四年。560頁。（Indian Diary.）

梶浦逸外（Kajiura, Itugai）光。インド佛跡めぐり。正眼寺。岐阜。昭和四十四年。195頁。（Pilgrimage to Indian Buddhist Monument.）

神坂次郎（Kamisaka, Jirou）天鼓鳴りやまず。北畠道竜の生涯。中公文庫。中央公論社。東京。1994。387頁。（Life of Kitabatake Doryu.）

加藤精神（Katou, Seisin）高丘親王の御事跡と御入竺の御年齢について。東洋大学紀要。通算3。東京。1942。（On Takaoka Shinno.）

北畠道竜（Kitabatake, Douryuu）天竺行路次所見。三巻。明治十九年。（Travelogue to India.）
明治文化全集。第7巻。外国文化編。日本評論社。東京。昭和3年。（Travelogue to India.）

佐伯有清（Sayeki, Yuusei）高丘親王入唐記。廃太子と虎害伝説の真相。吉川弘文館。東京。2002。（Prince Takaoka's Diary in Chinese Tang Dynasty.）

佐藤哲朗（Sato, Teturou）北畠道竜のブッダガヤ巡礼。大アジア思想活劇。

サンガ。東京。2008。(Kitabatake Doryu and Buddhagaya Pilgrimage.)

佐藤良純(Sato, Ryojun)ブッダガヤ寺院法をめぐって。パーリ学佛教文化学。第 1 巻。1998。pp. 121–134。(On Buddhagaya Temple Manegament Law.)

〃　佛伝をめぐる問題。大正大学学報。第七十七号。平成十四年。東京。pp. 43–48.(Essay on The Life of Buddha.)

里道徳雄(Satomichi, Tokuo)真如親王渡天にみる光と影。東洋学論集。通号 20。東京。1995。(Travels of Shinyo Shinno.)

静永孝英(Sizunaga, Kouei)インド聖地巡礼紀行。隆文館。東京。昭和四十七年。178 頁。(Indian Buddhist Sacred Places.)

杉本直次郎(Sugimoto, Naojiro)真如親王伝研究。吉川弘文館。東京。昭和 40 年。(Shinnyo Shinno.)

須田光夫(Suda, Mituo)インド佛跡巡礼紀行　内なる光を求めて。リーベル出版。東京。1999。242 頁。(Pilgrimage to India.)

スマナサーラ・アルボムツレ(Arbomure Sumanasara)ブッダの聖地。サンガ文庫。東京。2012。511 頁。(Sacred Places of Buddha.)

高楠順次郎(Takakusu, Junjiro)印度佛蹟実寫解説。巧芸社。東京。大正十五年。56 頁。(Pictures of Buddhist Remains in India.)

田中海量(Tanaka, Kairyo)インド佛蹟　いまむかし。現代における佛教と教化。ノンブル社。東京。pp. 33–56.(Buddhist Remains in India.)

田島公(Tajima, Kou)真如(高丘)親王一行の入唐の旅。頭陀親王入唐略記を読む。歴史と地理。502 号。山川出版社。1997。(Shinnyo (Takaoka)!s Travel to Chinese Tan Dynasty.)

中村元(Nakamura, Hajime)、奈良康明(Nara, Koumei)、佐藤良純(Sato, Ryojun)ブッダの世界。学習研究社。東京。1980。(再販)2000。(The World of Budddha.)

二橋進(Nihashi, Susumu)インド巡礼。釈尊の生涯をたどる。八雲書房。東京。昭和 51 年。328 頁。(Pilgrimage to India.)

森公章(Mori, Kousyou)遣外使節と求法・巡礼僧の日記。日本国際文化センター。(共同研報告)2011。pp. 339–353。(Pilgrimage Diary of Japanese Buddhist Priests.)

坂東性純(Bandou, Shoujun)、佐々木千洋(Sasaki, Senyou)、花山勝友(Hanayama, Shouyuu)。インド佛蹟巡礼紀行。東成出版社。東京。昭和三十年。五十頁。(Indian Buddhist Sacred Places.)

平等通昭(Byoudou, Tuushou)古き印度の旅。印度佛蹟紀行。仲光社。東京。昭和四十四年。233 頁。(Buddhist India.)

菩提樹学園の教育(Bodaiju Gakuen!s Kyouiku)国際佛教興隆協会。東京。2004。167 頁。(Education of Bodaijyu Gakuen.)

薬師寺(Yakushiji Temple)佛足跡。薬師寺。奈良。(Buddha's Foot Mark Stone of Yakusiji Temple.)

山本晋通(Yamamoto, Shintu)天竺紀行。是真会。諫早。昭和十六年。(Travel to India.)

BUDDHIST TRADITION SERIES

Gen. Ed. *ERNST STEINKELLNER*,
Joint Gen. Ed. *ALEXANDER VON ROSPATT*,
Founder Ed. Late *ALEX WAYMAN* [ISBN: 978-81-208-0287-2]

1 **Indian Buddhism**—*Hajime Nakamura*

2 **Nagarjuniana**—*Chr. Lindtner*

3 **Chinese Monks in India**—*Latika Lahiri*

4 **Buddhism in Central Asia**—*B.N. Puri*

5 **Dharmakīrti's Theory of Hetu- Centricity of Anumāna**—*Mangala R. Chinchore*

6 **The Legend of King Aśoka**—*John S. Strong*

7 **Buddhist Insight**—*George R. Elder*

8 **Buddhism Transformed**—*Richard Gombrich* and *Gananath Obeyesekere*

9 **The Buddhist Tantras**—*Alex Wayman*

10 **The Lion's Roar of Queen Śrīmālā**—*Alex Wayman* and *Hideko Wayman*

11 **The Buddha Nature**—*Brian E. Brown*

12 **Evolution of Stupas in Burma**—*Sujata Soni*

13 **Buddhist Parables**—*Eugene Watson Burlingame*

14 **The Debate of King Milinda**— *Bhikku Pesala*

15 **The Chinese Madhyama Āgama and the Pāli Majjhima Nikāya**—*Bhiksu Thich Minh Chau*

16 **Sudden and Gradual**—*Peter N. Gregory*

17 **Yoga of the Guhyasamājatantra**—*Alex Wayman*

18 **The Enlightenment of Vairocana**—*Alex Wayman* and *R. Tajima*

19 **A History of Indian Buddhism**—Tr. *Hirakawa Akira*, Ed. *Paul Groner*

20 **Introduction to the Buddhist Tantric Systems**—*F.D. Lessing* and *Alex Wayman*

21 **Anāgatavaṃsa Desanā**—Tr. *Udaya Meddegama*, Ed. *John C. Holt*

22 **Chinnamasta**—*Elisabeth Anne Benard*

23 **On Voidness** —*Fernando Tola* and *Carmen Dragonetti*

24 **Nāgārjuna's Refutation of Logic (Nyāya) Vaidalyaprakaraṇa**—*Fernando Tola* and *Carmen Dragonetti*

25 **The Buddhist Art of Nagarjunakonda**—*Elizabeth Rosen Stone*

26 **Discipline**—*J.C. Holt*

27 **Philosophy and its Development in the Nikāyas and Abhidhamma**—*Fumimaro Watanabe*

28 **Untying the Knots in Buddhism**—*Alex Wayman*

29 **Early Buddhist Theory of Knowledge**—*K.N. Jayatilleke*

30 **Calming the Mind and Discerning the Real**—Tr. *Alex Wayman*

31 **A Comparative Study of the Pratimoksha**—*W. Pachow*

32 **Rise of the Esoteric Buddhism in the Tibet**—*Eva M. Dargyay*

33-35 **Saṃyuktābhidharmahṛdaya (3 Parts)** *Bart Dessein*

36 **A Millennium of Buddhist Logic (Pt. I)**—*Alex Wayman*

37 **The Buddhist Pilgrimage**—*Duncan Forbes*

38 **Chanting the Name of Mañjuśrī**—*Alex Wayman*

39 **The Literature of the Personalists of Early Buddhism**—*Bhikshu Thich Thien Chau*

40 **The Laṅkāvatāra Sūtra** —*D.T. Suzuki*

41 **Studies in the Laṅkāvatāra Sūtra**—*D.T. Suzuki*

42 **The Vimalakīrti Sūtra**—*Burton Watson*

43 **The Gāndhārī Dharmapada**—*John Brough*

44 **Imaging Wisdom**—*Jacob N. Kinnard*

45 **Pain and Its Ending**—*Carol S. Anderson*

46 **Apparitions of the Self**—*Janet Gyatso*

47-49 **Rules for Nuns according to the Dharmaguptakavinya (3 Parts)**—*Ann Heirmann*

50 **The Chinese Hevajraṛantra**—*Ch. Willemen*

51 **The Historical Buddha**—*H.W. Schumann*, Tr. from the German *M.O'c Walshe*

52 **Dana:** Giving and Getting in Pali Buddhism—*Ellison Banks Findly*

53 **Hermeneutics and Tradition in the Samadhinirmocana Sutra**—*John Powers*

54 **Skillful Means**—*John W. Wchroeder.*

55 **The Two Truths in Chinese Buddhism**—*Chang-Qing Shih.*

56 **The Bodhisattva Path**—*Jan Nattier*

57 **Becoming the Buddha**—*Donald K. Swearer*

58 **Approaching the Land of Bliss**— Eds. *Richard K.Payne* & *Kenneth K. Tanaka*

59 **Indian Monastic Buddhism**—*Gregory Schopen*

60 **Caste and Buddhist Philosophy**—*Vincent Eltschinger*